THE
NEW TESTAMENT
DOCUMENTS

by

F. F. BRUCE, M.A., D.D., F.B.A.

*Formerly Rylands Professor of Biblical Criticism and Exegesis
in the University of Manchester*

Inter-Varsity Press,
Leicester, England

William B. Eerdmans Publishing Company
Grand Rapids, Michigan

Inter-Varsity Press
38 De Montfort Street, Leicester LE1 7GP, England
Wm. B. Eerdmans Publishing Company
255 Jefferson S.E., Grand Rapids, MI 49503

First published under the title
Are the New Testament Documents Reliable?

Fifth revised edition © The Inter-Varsity Fellowship

First Published 1943

Reprinted, December 1988

IVP EDITION 0 85110 307 3
EERDMANS EDITION 0-8028-1025-X

Printed in U.S.A. by Eerdmans Printing Company,
Grand Rapids, Michigan

Inter-Varsity Press is the publishing division of the Universities and Colleges Christian Fellowship (formerly the Inter-Varsity Fellowship), a student movement linking Christian Unions in universities and colleges throughout the United Kingdom and the Republic of Ireland, and a member movement of the International Fellowship of Evangelical Students. For information about local and national activities write to UCCF, 38 De Montfort Street, Leicester LE1 7GP.

CONTENTS

PREFACE TO THE FIFTH EDITION

'RELIABLE as what?' asked a discerning reviewer of the first edition of this little work, by way of a comment on the title. His point, I think, was that we should be concerned with the reliability of the New Testament as a witness to God's self-revelation in Christ rather than with its reliability as a record of historical fact. True; but the two questions are closely related. For, since Christianity claims to be a historical revelation, it is not irrelevant to look at its foundation documents from the standpoint of historical criticism.

When the first edition of this book (my literary first-born) appeared in 1943, I was a lecturer in classical studies, and had for long been accustomed to view the New Testament in its classical context. When I was invited from time to time to address audiences of sixth formers and university students on the trustworthiness of the New Testament in general and of the Gospel records in particular, my usual line was to show that the grounds for accepting the New Testament as trustworthy compared very favourably with the grounds on which classical students accepted the authenticity and credibility of many ancient documents. It was out of such talks that this book originally grew. It has (I am told) proved its usefulness to the readers for whom it was intended, not only in English-speaking lands but in German and Spanish translations as well.

The historical and philological lines of approach have, of course, their limitations. They cannot establish the Christian claim that the New Testament completes the inspired record of divine revelation. But non-theological students (for whom the book was written) are, in my experience, more ready to countenance such a claim for a work which is historically reliable than for one which is not. And I think they are right. It is, indeed, difficult to restrict a discussion of the New Testament writings

5

to the purely historical plane; theology insists on break-
ing in. But that is as it should be; history and theology
are inextricably intertwined in the gospel of our salvation, which owes its eternal and universal validity to
certain events which happened in Palestine when
Tiberius ruled the Roman Empire.

I welcome the opportunity to give the book a
thorough revision (not thorough enough, some of my
friends may think); and in sending it forth afresh I
continue to dedicate it to those university and college
students throughout the world who, singly or in groups,
maintain among their colleagues the apostolic witness to
Jesus Christ our Lord.

F. F. B.

April 1959.

PREFACE TO SIXTH EDITION

It is nearly forty years since this little book was first written,
and over twenty years since it received its last thorough-
going revision. Since then minor changes have been made
from one printing to the next, to keep it reasonably up to
date, and that is all that has been done this time. It is
gratifying to be assured that the book still helps to serve
the purpose for which it was written. It is, I am sure, a better book for that purpose than any that I could write today,
so I send it forth again, dedicated, as before, to Christian
students throughout the world.

F.F.B.

December 1981

CHAPTER 1

DOES IT MATTER?

DOES it matter whether the New Testament documents are reliable or not? Is it so very important that we should be able to accept them as truly historical records? Some people will very confidently return a negative answer to both these questions. The fundamental principles of Christianity, they say, are laid down in the Sermon on the Mount and elsewhere in the New Testament; their validity is not affected by the truth or falsehood of the narrative framework in which they are set. Indeed, it may be that we know nothing certain about the Teacher into whose mouth they are put; the story of Jesus as it has come down to us may be myth or legend, but the teaching ascribed to Him—whether He was actually responsible for it or not—has a value all its own, and a man who accepts and follows that teaching can be a true Christian even if he believes that Christ never lived at all.

This argument sounds plausible, and it may be applicable to some religions. It might be held, for example, that the ethics of Confucianism have an independent value quite apart from the story of the life of Confucius himself, just as the philosophy of Plato must be considered on its own merits, quite apart from the traditions that have come down to us about the life of Plato and the question of the extent of his indebtedness to Socrates. But the argument can be applied to the New Testament only if we ignore the real essence of Christianity. For the Christian gospel is not primarily a code of ethics or a metaphysical system; it is first and foremost good news, and as such it was proclaimed by its earliest preachers. True, they called Christianity 'The Way'[1] and 'The Life';[2] but Christianity as a way of life depends upon the

[1] Cf. Acts ix. 2, xix. 9, 23, xxii. 4, xxiv. 14, 22.
[2] Cf. Acts v. 20.

7

acceptance of Christianity as good news. And this good news is intimately bound up with the historical order, for it tells how for the world's redemption God entered into history, the eternal came into time, the kingdom of heaven invaded the realm of earth, in the great events of the incarnation, crucifixion, and resurrection of Jesus the Christ. The first recorded words of our Lord's public preaching in Galilee are : 'The time is fulfilled, and the kingdom of God has drawn near; repent and believe the good news.'[1]

That Christianity has its roots in history is emphasized in the Church's earliest creeds, which fix the supreme revelation of God at a particular point in time, when 'Jesus Christ, His only Son our Lord . . . suffered under Pontius Pilate'. This historical 'once-for-all-ness' of Christianity, which distinguishes it from those religious and philosophical systems which are not specially related to any particular time, makes the reliability of the writings which purport to record this revelation a question of first-rate importance.

It may be replied that while admittedly the truth of the Christian faith is bound up closely with the historicity of the New Testament, the question of the historicity of this record is of little importance for those who on other grounds deny the truth of Christianity. The Christian might answer that the historicity of the New Testament and the truth of Christianity do not become less vitally important for mankind by being ignored or denied. But the truth of the New Testament documents is also a very important question on purely historical grounds. The words of the historian Lecky, who was no believer in revealed religion, have often been quoted :

'The character of Jesus has not only been the highest pattern of virtue, but the strongest incentive to its practice, and has exerted so deep an influence, that it may be truly said, that the simple record of three short years of active life has done more to regenerate and to soften mankind, than all the disquisitions of philosophers and than all the exhortations of moralists.'[2]

---

[1] See Mk. i. 15.
[2] W. E. H. Lecky, *History of European Morals*, ii (1869), p. 88.

But the character of Jesus can be known only from the New Testament records; the influence of His character is therefore tantamount to the influence of the New Testament records. Would it not, then, be paradoxical if the records which, on the testimony of a rationalist historian, produced such results, were devoid of historical truth? This, of course, does not in itself prove the historicity of these records, for history is full of paradoxes, but it does afford an additional reason for seriously investigating the trustworthiness of records which have had so marked an influence on human history. Whether our approach is theological or historical, it does matter whether the New Testament documents are reliable or not.[1]

[1] It is, perhaps, not superfluous to remark that before going on to consider the trustworthiness of the New Testament writings, it would be a good idea to read them!

CHAPTER 2

THE NEW TESTAMENT DOCUMENTS: THEIR DATE AND ATTESTATION

1. *What are the New Testament documents?*

THE New Testament as we know it consists of twenty-seven short Greek writings, commonly called 'books', the first five of which are historical in character, and are thus of more immediate concern for our present study. Four of these we call the Gospels, because each of them narrates the gospel—the good news that God revealed Himself in Jesus Christ for the redemption of mankind. All four relate sayings and doings of Christ, but can scarcely be called biographies in our modern sense of the word, as they deal almost exclusively with the last two or three years of His life, and devote what might seem a disproportionate space to the week immediately preceding His death. They are not intended to be 'Lives' of Christ, but rather to present from distinctive points of view, and originally for different publics, the good news concerning Him. The first three Gospels (those according to Matthew, Mark and Luke), because of certain features which link them together, are commonly called the 'Synoptic Gospels'.[1]

The fifth historical writing, the Acts of the Apostles, is actually a continuation of the third Gospel, written by the same author, Luke the physician and companion of the apostle Paul. It gives us an account of the rise of Christianity after the resurrection and ascension of Christ, and of its extension in a westerly direction from Palestine to Rome, within about thirty years of the crucifixion. Of the other writings twenty-one are letters. Thirteen of these bear the name of Paul, nine of them being addressed to churches[2] and four to individuals.[3]

[1] See pp. 29 ff.

[2] The Epistles to the Romans, 1 and 2 Corinthians, Galatians, Ephesians, Philippians, Colossians, 1 and 2 Thessalonians.

[3] The Epistles to Philemon, 1 and 2 Timothy, Titus.

Another letter, the Epistle to the Hebrews, is anonymous, but was at an early date bound up with the Pauline Epistles, and came to be frequently ascribed to Paul. It was probably written shortly before AD 70 to a community of Jewish Christians in Italy. Of the remaining letters one bears the name of James, probably the brother of our Lord; one of Jude, who calls himself the brother of James; two of Peter; and there are three which bear no name, but because of their obvious affinities with the fourth Gospel have been known from early days as the Epistles of John. The remaining book is the Apocalypse, or book of the Revelation.[1] It belongs to a literary *genre* which, though strange to our minds, was well known in Jewish and Christian circles in those days, the apocalyptic.[2] The Revelation is introduced by seven covering letters, addressed to seven churches in the province of Asia. The author, John by name, was at the time exiled on the island of Patmos in the Ægean Sea, and reports a series of visions which symbolically portray the triumph of Christ both in His own passion and in the sufferings of His people at the hand of His enemies and theirs. The book was written in the days of the Flavian emperors (AD 69-96) to encourage hard-pressed Christians with the assurance that, notwithstanding the apparent odds against which they had to contend, their victory was not in doubt; Jesus, not Caesar, had been invested by the Almighty with the sovereignty of the world.

Of these twenty-seven books, then, we are chiefly concerned at present with the first five, which are cast in narrative form, though the others, and especially the letters of Paul, are important for our purpose in so far as they contain historical allusions or otherwise throw light on the Gospels and Acts.

2. *What are the dates of these documents?*
The crucifixion of Christ took place, it is generally agreed, about AD 30. According to Luke iii. 1, the

---

[1] *N.B.*—Revelation (singular); *not* Revelations (plural).

[2] From Greek *apokalyptein*, 'to unveil'. The earliest example of this *genre* is the Old Testament book of Daniel.

activity of John the Baptist, which immediately preceded the commencement of our Lord's public ministry, is dated in 'the fifteenth year of Tiberius Cæsar'. Now, Tiberius became emperor in August, AD 14, and according to the method of computation current in Syria, which Luke would have followed, his fifteenth year commenced in September or October, AD 27.[1] The fourth Gospel mentions three Passovers after this time;[2] the third Passover from that date would be the Passover of AD 30, at which it is probable on other grounds that the crucifixion took place. At this time, too, we know from other sources that Pilate was Roman governor of Judæa, Herod Antipas was tetrarch of Galilee, and Caiaphas was Jewish high priest.[3]

The New Testament was complete, or substantially complete, about AD 100, the majority of the writings being in existence twenty to forty years before this. In this country a majority of modern scholars fix the dates of the four Gospels as follows: Matthew, *c.* 85-90; Mark, *c.* 65; Luke, *c.* 80-85; John, *c.* 90-100.[4] I should be inclined to date the first three Gospels rather earlier: Mark around AD 64 or 65, Luke shortly before 70, and Matthew shortly after 70. One criterion which has special weight with me is the relation which these writings appear to bear to the destruction of the city and temple of Jerusalem by the Romans in AD 70. My view of the matter is that Mark and Luke were written before this event, and Matthew not long afterwards.

[1] The method in Syria, retained from the days of the Seleucid kings, was to reckon the start of a new regnal year in September-October. As Tiberius became emperor in August, AD 14, his second regnal year would thus be regarded as beginning in September-October of the same year. The Passover of Jn. ii. 13 ff. accordingly was that of March, AD 28, and this agrees with the chronological indication of ii. 20, for Herod's temple was commenced in 20-19 BC, and 46 years from that brings us to AD 27-28.

[2] Jn. ii. 13, vi. 4, xi. 55 ff.

[3] See Chapters ix and x.

[4] As, for example, B. H. Streeter in *The Four Gospels* (1924), and V. Taylor in *The Gospels* (1945). Arguments for an earlier dating will be found in A. Harnack, *The Date of the Acts and the Synoptic Gospels* (1911); C. E. Raven, *Jesus and the Gospel of Love* (1931), pp. 128 ff.; J. A. T. Robinson, *Redating the New Testament* (1976).

But even with the later dates, the situation is encouraging from the historian's point of view, for the first three Gospels were written at a time when many were alive who could remember the things that Jesus said and did, and some at least would still be alive when the fourth Gospel was written. If it could be determined that the writers of the Gospels used sources of information belonging to an earlier date, then the situation would be still more encouraging. But a more detailed examination of the Gospels will come in a later chapter.

The date of the writing of Acts will depend on the date we affix to the third Gospel, for both are parts of one historical work, and the second part appears to have been written soon after the first. There are strong arguments for dating the twofold work not long after Paul's two years' detention in Rome (AD 60-62).[1] Some scholars, however, consider that the 'former treatise' to which Acts originally formed the sequel was not our present Gospel of Luke but an earlier draft, sometimes called 'Proto-Luke'; this enables them to date Acts in the sixties, while holding that the Gospel of Luke in its final form was rather later.[2]

The dates of the thirteen Pauline Epistles can be fixed partly by internal and partly by external evidence. The day has gone by when the authenticity of these letters could be denied wholesale. There are some writers today who would reject Ephesians; fewer would reject 2 Thessalonians; more would deny that the Pastoral Epistles (1 and 2 Timothy and Titus) came in their present form from the hand of Paul.[3] I accept them all as Pauline, but the remaining eight letters would by themselves be sufficient for our purpose, and it is from these that the main arguments are drawn in our later chapter on 'The Importance of Paul's Evidence'.

Ten of the letters which bear Paul's name belong to the period before the end of his Roman imprisonment.

[1] Acts xxviii. 30. See F. F. Bruce, *The Book of the Acts* (1954), pp. 21 ff.

[2] *Cf.* C. S. C. Williams, *A Commentary on the Acts of the Apostles* (1957), pp. 13 ff.

[3] *Cf.* D. Guthrie, *The Pastoral Epistles* (1957), pp. 11 ff.

These ten, in order of writing, may be dated as follows: Galatians, 48[1]; 1 and 2 Thessalonians, 50; 1 and 2 Corinthians, 54-56; Romans, 57; Philippians, Colossians, Philemon, and Ephesians, c. 60. The Pastoral Epistles, in their diction and historical atmosphere, contain signs of later date than the other Pauline Epistles, but this presents less difficulty to those who believe in a second imprisonment of Paul at Rome about the year 65, which was ended by his execution.[3] The Pastoral Epistles can then be dated c. 63-65, and the changed state of affairs in the Pauline churches to which they bear witness will have been due in part to the opportunity which Paul's earlier Roman imprisonment afforded to his opponents in these churches.

At any rate, the time elapsing between the evangelic events and the writing of most of the New Testament books was, from the standpoint of historical research, satisfactorily short. For in assessing the trustworthiness of ancient historical writings, one of the most important questions is : How soon after the events took place were they recorded?

3. *What is the evidence for their early existence?*

About the middle of the last century it was confidently asserted by a very influential school of thought that some of the most important books of the New Testament, including the Gospels and the Acts, did not exist before the thirties of the second century AD.[4] This conclusion

---

[1] On the view that it was written before the Council of Jerusalem of Acts xv; others would date it a few years later.

[2] On the view that it was written during Paul's Roman imprisonment; when one of his hearers, a student of history, interposed with the protest, 'But, Herr Professor, the facts are otherwise.' ment; others would date it from Ephesus about AD 55.

[3] *Cf.* Eusebius, *Hist. Eccl.* ii. 22, 25.

[4] The 'Tübingen' school, so called from the University of Tübingen, where F. C. Baur, the leading exponent of these views, was Professor. This school restated the origins of Christianity in terms of Hegelian metaphysics. Their methods exemplified the attitude summed up in a famous classroom story, which tells how Hegel was propounding his philosophy of history with reference to a particular series of events, when one of his hearers, a student of history, interposed with the protest, 'But, Herr Professor, the facts are otherwise.' 'So much the worse for the facts,' said Hegel.

These theories were popularized in this country in 1874 by the 'anonymous' author of *Supernatural Religion* (Walter R. Cassels),

was the result not so much of historical evidence as of philosophical presuppositions. Even then there was sufficient historical evidence to show how unfounded these theories were, as Lightfoot, Tischendorf, Tregelles and others demonstrated in their writings; but the amount of such evidence available in our own day is so much greater and more conclusive that a first-century date for most of the New Testament writings cannot reasonably be denied, no matter what our philosophical presuppositions may be.

The evidence for our New Testament writings is ever so much greater than the evidence for many writings of classical authors, the authenticity of which no-one dreams of questioning. And if the New Testament were a collection of secular writings, their authenticity would generally be regarded as beyond all doubt. It is a curious fact that historians have often been much readier to trust the New Testament records than have many theologians.[1] Somehow or other, there are people who regard a 'sacred book' as *ipso facto* under suspicion, and demand much more corroborative evidence for such a work than they would for an ordinary secular or pagan writing. From the viewpoint of the historian, the same standards must be applied to both. But we do not quarrel with those who want more evidence for the New Testament than for other writings; firstly, because the universal claims which the New Testament makes upon mankind are so absolute, and the character and works of its chief Figure so unparalleled, that we want to be as sure of its truth as we possibly can; and secondly, because in point of fact there *is* much more evidence for the New Testament than for other ancient writings of comparable date.

which was answered by Bishop Lightfoot in articles in the *Contemporary Review*, 1874-77, reprinted in the volume *Essays on 'Supernatural Religion'* (1889). Cassels' thesis and Lightfoot's reply may be specially recommended to students of logic who are interested in the validity of the 'argument from silence'.

[1] *Cf.* A. N. Sherwin-White, *Roman Society and Roman Law in the New Testament* (1963), p. 189, for the surprised reaction of a classical historian to 'basic assumptions of form-criticism of the extremer sort'.

There are in existence over 5,000 Greek manuscripts of the New Testament in whole or in part. The best and most important of these go back to somewhere about AD 350, the two most important being the Codex Vaticanus, the chief treasure of the Vatican Library in Rome, and the well-known Codex Sinaiticus, which the British Government purchased from the Soviet Government for £100,000 on Christmas Day, 1933, and which is now the chief treasure of the British Museum. Two other important early MSS in this country are the Codex Alexandrinus, also in the British Museum, written in the fifth century, and the Codex Bezæ, in Cambridge University Library, written in the fifth or sixth century, and containing the Gospels and Acts in both Greek and Latin.

Perhaps we can appreciate how wealthy the New Testament is in manuscript attestation if we compare the textual material for other ancient historical works. For Cæsar's *Gallic War* (composed between 58 and 50 BC) there are several extant MSS, but only nine or ten are good, and the oldest is some 900 years later than Cæsar's day. Of the 142 books of the Roman History of Livy (59 BC-AD 17) only thirty-five survive; these are known to us from not more than twenty MSS of any consequence, only one of which, and that containing fragments of Books iii-vi, is as old as the fourth century. Of the fourteen books of the *Histories* of Tacitus (*c.* AD 100) only four and a half survive; of the sixteen books of his *Annals,* ten survive in full and two in part. The text of these extant portions of his two great historical works depends entirely on two MSS, one of the ninth century and one of the eleventh. The extant MSS of his minor works (*Dialogus de Oratoribus, Agricola, Germania*) all descend from a codex of the tenth century. The History of Thucydides (*c.* 460-400 BC) is known to us from eight MSS, the earliest belonging to *c.* AD 900, and a few papyrus scraps, belonging to about the beginning of the Christian era. The same is true of the History of Herodotus (*c.* 488-428 BC). Yet no classical scholar would listen to an argument that the authenticity of Herodotus or Thucydides is in doubt because the earliest

MSS of their works which are of any use to us are over 1,300 years later than the originals.

But how different is the situation of the New Testament in this respect! In addition to the two excellent MSS of the fourth century mentioned above, which are the earliest of some thousands known to us, considerable fragments remain of papyrus copies of books of the New Testament dated from 100 to 200 years earlier still. The Chester Beatty Biblical Papyri, the existence of which was made public in 1931, consist of portions of eleven papyrus codices, three of which contained most of the New Testament writings. One of these, containing the four Gospels with Acts, belongs to the first half of the third century; another, containing Paul's letters to churches and the Epistle to the Hebrews, was copied at the beginning of the third century; the third, containing Revelation, belongs to the second half of the same century.

A more recent discovery consists of some papyrus fragments dated by papyrological experts not later than AD 150, published in *Fragments of an Unknown Gospel and other Early Christian Papyri*, by H. I. Bell and T. C. Skeat (1935). These fragments contain what has been thought by some to be portions of a fifth Gospel having strong affinities with the canonical four; but much more probable is the view expressed in *The Times Literary Supplement* for 25 April 1935, 'that these fragments were written by someone who had the four Gospels before him and knew them well; that they did not profess to be an independent Gospel; but were paraphrases of the stories and other matter in the Gospels designed for explanation and instruction, a manual to teach people the Gospel stories'.

Earlier still is a fragment of a papyrus codex containing John xviii. 31-33, 37 f., now in the John Rylands Library, Manchester, dated on palaeographical grounds around AD 130, showing that the latest of the four Gospels, which was written, according to tradition, at Ephesus between AD 90 and 100, was circulating in Egypt within about forty years of its composition (if, as is most likely, this papyrus originated in Egypt, where it was acquired in 1917). It must be regarded as being, by half a century, the earliest extant fragment of the New Testament.[1]

A more recently discovered papyrus manuscript of the same Gospel, while not so early as the Rylands papyrus, is incomparably better preserved; this is the Papyrus Bodmer II, whose discovery was announced by the Bodmer Library of Geneva in 1956; it was written about AD 200, and contains the first fourteen chapters of the Gospel of John with but one lacuna (of twenty-two verses), and considerable portions of the last seven chapters.[2]

Attestation of another kind is provided by allusions to and quotations from the New Testament books in other early writings. The authors known as the Apostolic Fathers wrote chiefly between AD 90 and 160, and in their works we find evidence for their acquaintance with most of the books of the New Testament. In three works whose date is probably round about AD 100—the 'Epistle of Barnabas', written perhaps in Alexandria; the *Didache*, or 'Teaching of the Twelve Apostles', produced somewhere in Syria or Palestine; and the letter sent to the Corinthian church by Clement, bishop of Rome, about AD 96—we find fairly certain quotations from the common tradition of the Synoptic Gospels, from Acts, Romans, 1 Corinthians, Ephesians, Titus, Hebrews, 1 Peter, and possible quotations from other books of the New Testament. In the letters written by Ignatius, bishop of Antioch, as he journeyed to his martyrdom in Rome in AD 115, there are reasonably identifiable quotations from Matthew, John, Romans, 1 and 2 Corinthians, Galatians, Ephesians, Philippians, 1 and 2 Timothy, Titus, and possible allusions to Mark, Luke, Acts, Colossians, 2 Thessalonians, Philemon, Hebrews, and 1 Peter. His younger contemporary, Polycarp, in a letter to the Philippians (*c.* 120) quotes from the common tradition of the Synoptic Gospels, from Acts, Romans, 1 and 2 Corinthians, Galatians, Ephesians, Philippians, 2 Thessalonians, 1 and 2 Timothy, Hebrews,

[1] For the text and description of the papyrus see C. H. Roberts, *An Unpublished Fragment of the Fourth Gospel* (1935).   [2] See p.20.

1 Peter, and 1 John. And so we might go on through the writers of the second century, amassing increasing evidence of their familiarity with and recognition of the authority of the New Testament writings. So far as the Apostolic Fathers are concerned, the evidence is collected and weighed in a work called *The New Testament in the Apostolic Fathers,* recording the findings of a committee of the Oxford Society of Historical Theology in 1905.

Nor is it only in orthodox Christian writers that we find evidence of this sort. It is evident from the recently discovered writings of the Gnostic school of Valentinus that before the middle of the second century most of the New Testament books were as well known and as fully venerated in that heretical circle as they were in the Catholic Church.[1]

The study of the kind of attestation found in MSS and quotations in later writers is connected with the approach known as Textual Criticism.[2] This is a most important and fascinating branch of study, its object being to determine as exactly as possible from the available evidence the original words of the documents in question. It is easily proved by experiment that it is difficult to copy out a passage of any considerable length without making one or two slips at least. When we have documents like our New Testament writings copied and recopied thousands of times, the scope for copyists' errors is so enormously increased that it is surprising there are no more than there actually are. Fortunately, if the great number of MSS increases the number of scribal errors, it increases proportionately the means of correcting such errors, so that the margin of doubt left in the process of recovering the exact original wording is not so large as might be feared; it is in truth remarkably small. The variant readings about which any doubt

[1] See F. L. Cross (ed.), *The Jung Codex* (1955), pp. 81 ff. *Cf.* pp. 98 f. below.

[2] Another very important class of witnesses to the text of the New Testament are the Ancient Versions in other languages, the oldest of which, the Old Syriac and the Old Latin, go back to the latter half of the second century. Valuable help can also be derived from early Church lectionaries.

remains among textual critics of the New Testament affect no material question of historic fact or of Christian faith and practice.

To sum up, we may quote the verdict of the late Sir Frederic Kenyon, a scholar whose authority to make pronouncements on ancient MSS was second to none :

> 'The interval then between the dates of original composition and the earliest extant evidence becomes so small as to be in fact negligible, and the last foundation for any doubt that the Scriptures have come down to us substantially as they were written has now been removed. Both the *authenticity* and the *general integrity* of the books of the New Testament may be regarded as finally established.'[1]

[1] *The Bible and Archæology* (1940), pp. 288 f.

Additional Note to p. 18: Other Bodmer papyri announced more recently include a codex of *c.* AD 200 containing parts of Luke and John, another of the same approximate date containing the Epistles of Peter and Jude, and one of the sixth or seventh century containing Acts and the General Epistles.

Additional Note to p. 20: The latest exhaustive enquiry into the dates of the New Testament books – *Redating the New Testament*, by J. A. T. Robinson (1976) – argues that everything in the New Testament was written before AD 70, the latest book being Revelation, which he dates preferably under Galba (June 68–January 69). The pivot of his case is the Gospel of John, to the final form of which he gives a date no later than AD 65. I should not go all the way with some of his early dating, for I believe that one or two of the New Testament documents do imply that the fall of Jerusalem (AD 70) had already taken place. But Dr. Robinson's case is so well researched and closely reasoned that no-one from now on should deal with this question of dating without paying the most serious attention to his arguments.

CHAPTER 3

THE CANON OF
THE NEW TESTAMENT

EVEN when we have come to a conclusion about the date and origin of the individual books of the New Testament, another question remains to be answered. How did the New Testament itself as a collection of writings come into being? Who collected the writings, and on what principles? What circumstances led to the fixing of a list, or *canon,* of authoritative books?

The historic Christian belief is that the Holy Spirit, who controlled the writing of the individual books, also controlled their selection and collection, thus continuing to fulfil our Lord's promise that He would guide His disciples into all the truth. This, however, is something that is to be discerned by spiritual insight, and not by historical research. Our object is to find out what historical research reveals about the origin of the New Testament canon. Some will tell us that we receive the twenty-seven books of the New Testament on the authority of the Church; but even if we do, how did the Church come to recognize these twenty-seven and no others as worthy of being placed on a level of inspiration and authority with the Old Testament canon?

The matter is over-simplified in Article VI of the Thirty-Nine Articles, when it says : 'In the name of the holy Scripture we do understand those canonical Books of the Old and New Testament, of whose authority was never any doubt in the Church.' For, leaving on one side the question of the Old Testament canon, it is not quite accurate to say that there has *never* been *any* doubt in the Church of *any* of our New Testament books. A few of the shorter Epistles (*e.g.* 2 Peter, 2 and 3 John, James, Jude) and the Revelation were much longer in being accepted in some parts than in others;

while elsewhere books which we do not now include in the New Testament were received as canonical. Thus the Codex Sinaiticus included the 'Epistle of Barnabas' and the *Shepherd* of Hermas, a Roman work of about AD 110 or earlier, while the Codex Alexandrinus included the writings known as the First and Second Epistles of Clement; and the inclusion of these works alongside the biblical writings probably indicates that they were accorded some degree of canonical status.

The earliest list of New Testament books of which we have definite knowledge was drawn up at Rome by the heretic Marcion about 140. Marcion distinguished the inferior Creator-God of the Old Testament from the God and Father revealed in Christ, and believed that the Church ought to jettison all that appertained to the former. This 'theological anti-Semitism' involved the rejecting not only of the entire Old Testament but also of those parts of the New Testament which seemed to him to be infected with Judaism. So Marcion's canon consisted of two parts : (*a*) an expurgated edition of the third Gospel, which is the least Jewish of the Gospels, being written by the Gentile Luke; and (*b*) ten of the Pauline Epistles (the three 'Pastoral Epistles' being omitted). Marcion's list, however, does not represent the current verdict of the Church but a deliberate aberration from it.

Another early list, also of Roman provenance, dated about the end of the second century, is that commonly called the 'Muratorian Fragment', because it was first published in Italy in 1740 by the antiquarian Cardinal L. A. Muratori. It is unfortunately mutilated at the beginning, but it evidently mentioned Matthew and Mark, because it refers to Luke as the third Gospel; then it mentions John, Acts, Paul's nine letters to churches and four to individuals (Philemon, Titus, 1 and 2 Timothy),[1] Jude, two Epistles of John,[2] and the

---

[1] It adds that other letters circulating under Paul's name were not accepted by the Church. These were mainly pseudepigrapha composed in heretical interests.

[2] At this point it curiously adds the *Wisdom of Solomon*.

Apocalypse of John and that of Peter.[1] The *Shepherd of Hermas* is mentioned as worthy to be read (*i.e.* in church) but not to be included in the number of prophetic or apostolic writings.

The first steps in the formation of a canon of authoritative Christian books, worthy to stand beside the Old Testament canon, which was the Bible of our Lord and His apostles, appear to have been taken about the beginning of the second century, when there is evidence for the circulation of two collections of Christian writings in the Church.

At a very early date it appears that the four Gospels were united in one collection. They must have been brought together very soon after the writing of the Gospel according to John. This fourfold collection was known originally as 'The Gospel' in the singular, not 'The Gospels' in the plural; there was only one Gospel, narrated in four records, distinguished as 'according to Matthew', 'according to Mark', and so on. About AD 115 Ignatius, bishop of Antioch, refers to 'The Gospel' as an authoritative writing, and as he knew more than one of the four 'Gospels' it may well be that by 'The Gospel' *sans phrase* he means the fourfold collection which went by that name.

About AD 170 an Assyrian Christian named Tatian turned the fourfold Gospel into a continuous narrative or 'Harmony of the Gospels', which for long was the favourite if not the official form of the fourfold Gospel in the Assyrian Church. It was distinct from the four Gospels in the Old Syriac version.[2] It is not certain whether Tatian originally composed his Harmony, usually known as the *Diatessaron,* in Greek or in Syriac; but as it seems to have been compiled at Rome its original language was probably Greek, and a fragment of Tatian's *Diatessaron* in Greek was discovered in the year 1933 at Dura-Europos on the Euphrates. At any

[1] This apocryphal 'Apocalypse of Peter', says the fragment, some refuse to have read in church. We know from Clement, Eusebius, and Sozomen that it was read in some churches. For the extant fragments of this Apocalypse, see M. R. James' *Apocryphal N.T.*, pp. 505 ff.

[2] See p. 19, n. 2.

rate, it was given to the Assyrian Christians in a Syriac form when Tatian returned home from Rome, and this Syriac *Diatessaron* remained the 'Authorized Version' of the Gospels for them until it was replaced by the Peshitta or 'simple' version in the fifth century.

By the time of Irenæus, who, though a native of Asia Minor, was bishop of Lyons in Gaul about AD 180, the idea of a fourfold Gospel had become so axiomatic in the Church at large that he can refer to it as an established and recognized fact as obvious as the four cardinal points or the four winds:

> 'For as there are four quarters of the world in which we live, and four universal winds, and as the Church is dispersed over all the earth, and the gospel is the pillar and base of the Church and the breath of life, so it is natural that it should have four pillars, breathing immortality from every quarter and kindling the life of men anew. Whence it is manifest that the Word, the architect of all things, who sits upon the cherubim and holds all things together, having been manifested to men, has given us the gospel in fourfold form, but held together by one Spirit.'[1]

When the four Gospels were gathered together in one volume, it meant the severance of the two parts of Luke's history. When Luke and Acts were thus separated, one or two modifications were apparently introduced into the text at the end of Luke and the beginning of Acts. Originally Luke seems to have left all mention of the ascension to his second treatise; now the words 'and was carried up into heaven' were added in Luke xxiv. 51, to round off the narrative, and in consequence 'was taken up' was added in Acts i. 2. Thus the inconcinnities which some have detected between the accounts of the ascension in Luke and Acts are most likely due to these adjustments made when the two books were separated from each other.[2]

Acts, however, naturally shared the authority and prestige of the third Gospel, being the work of the same author, and was apparently received as canonical by all

---

[1] *Adv. Haer.* iii. 11, 8.
[2] *Cf.* F. F. Bruce, *The Acts of the Apostles* (Tyndale Press, 1951), pp. 66 f.

except Marcion and his followers. Indeed, Acts occupied a very important place in the New Testament canon, being the pivotal book of the New Testament, as Harnack called it, since it links the Gospels with the Epistles, and, by its record of the conversion, call, and missionary service of Paul, showed clearly how real an apostolic authority lay behind the Pauline Epistles.

The *corpus Paulinum*, or collection of Paul's writings, was brought together about the same time as the collecting of the fourfold Gospel.[1] As the Gospel collection was designated by the Greek word *Euangelion*, so the Pauline collection was designated by the one word *Apostolos*, each letter being distinguished as 'To the Romans', 'First to the Corinthians', and so on. Before long, the anonymous Epistle to the Hebrews was bound up with the Pauline writings. Acts, as a matter of convenience, came to be bound up with the 'General Epistles' (those of Peter, James, John and Jude).

The only books about which there was any substantial doubt after the middle of the second century were some of those which come at the end of our New Testament. Origen (185-254) mentions the four Gospels, the Acts, the thirteen Paulines, 1 Peter, 1 John and Revelation as acknowledged by all; he says that Hebrews, 2 Peter, 2 and 3 John, James and Jude, with the 'Epistle of Barnabas', the *Shepherd* of Hermas, the *Didache*, and the 'Gospel according to the Hebrews', were disputed by some. Eusebius (*c.* 265-340) mentions as generally acknowledged all the books of our New Testament except James, Jude, 2 Peter, 2 and 3 John, which were disputed by some, but recognized by the majority.[2] Athanasius in 367 lays down the twenty-seven books of our New Testament as alone canonical; shortly afterwards Jerome and Augustine followed his example in the West. The process farther east took a little longer;

---

[1] Ignatius and Polycarp (writing *c.* AD 115) seem to be acquainted with collections of Paul's Epistles. 2 Pet. iii. 15 f. seems to testify to a collection of at least some Pauline Epistles (the date of 2 Peter is disputed, but if it is alluded to in the 'Epistle of Barnabas', that would make it earlier than that work).

[2] Eusebius himself would have liked to reject the Apocalypse, because he disliked its millenarianism.

it was not until *c.* 508 that 2 Peter, 2 and 3 John, Jude and Revelation were included in a version of the Syriac Bible in addition to the other twenty-two books.

For various reasons it was necessary for the Church to know exactly what books were divinely authoritative. The Gospels, recording 'all that Jesus began both to do and to teach', could not be regarded as one whit lower in authority than the Old Testament books. And the teaching of the apostles in the Acts and Epistles was regarded as vested with His authority. It was natural, then, to accord to the apostolic writings of the new covenant the same degree of homage as was already paid to the prophetic writings of the old. Thus Justin Martyr, about AD 150, classes the 'Memoirs of the Apostles' along with the writings of the prophets, saying that both were read in meetings of Christians (*Apol.* i. 67). For the Church did not, in spite of the breach with Judaism, repudiate the authority of the Old Testament, but, following the example of Christ and His apostles, received it as the Word of God. Indeed, so much did they make the Septuagint their own that, although it was originally a translation of the Hebrew Scriptures into Greek for Greek-speaking Jews before the time of Christ, the Jews left the Septuagint to the Christians, and a fresh Greek version of the Old Testament was made for Greek-speaking Jews.

It was specially important to determine which books might be used for the establishment of Christian doctrine, and which might most confidently be appealed to in disputes with heretics. In particular, when Marcion drew up his canon about AD 140, it was necessary for the orthodox churches to know exactly what the true canon was, and this helped to speed up a process which had already begun. It is wrong, however, to talk or write as if the Church first began to draw up a canon after Marcion had published his.

Other circumstances which demanded clear definition of those books which possessed divine authority were the necessity of deciding which books should be read in church services (though certain books might be suitable for this purpose which could not be used to settle doctrinal questions), and the necessity of knowing which books might and might not be handed over on demand to the imperial police in times of persecution without incurring the guilt of sacrilege.

One thing must be emphatically stated. The New Testament books did not become authoritative for the Church because they were formally included in a canonical list; on the contrary, the Church included them in her canon because she already regarded them as divinely inspired, recognizing their innate worth and generally apostolic authority, direct or indirect. The first ecclesiastical councils to classify the canonical books were both held in North Africa—at Hippo Regius in 393 and at Carthage in 397—but what these councils did was not to impose something new upon the Christian communities but to codify what was already the general practice of those communities.

There are many theological questions arising out of the history of the canon which we cannot go into here; but for a practical demonstration that the Church made the right choice one need only compare the books of our New Testament with the various early documents collected by M. R. James in his *Apocryphal New Testament* (1924), or even with the writings of the Apostolic Fathers,[1] to realize the superiority of our New Testament books to these others.[2]

A word may be added about the 'Gospel according to the Hebrews' which, as was mentioned above, Origen listed as one of the books which in his day were disputed by some. This work, which circulated in Transjordan and Egypt among the Jewish-Christian groups called Ebionites, bore some affinity to the canonical Gospel of Matthew. Perhaps it was an independent expansion of

---

[1] The writings of the Apostolic Fathers, in Greek and English, are available in one volume, edited by J. B. Lightfoot (Macmillan, 1891), and in two volumes of the Loeb Classical Library, edited by Kirsopp Lake (Heinemann, 1912-13). Although they represent a decline from the New Testament level, they are much superior to the apocryphal Gospels and Acts.

[2] I have discussed this subject of canonicity more fully in *The Books and the Parchments* (1963), pp. 95 ff., in *The Spreading Flame* (1958), pp. 221 ff., and in *Tradition Old and New* (1970), pp. 129 ff.

an Aramaic document related to our canonical Matthew; it was known to some of the early Christian Fathers in a Greek version.

Jerome (347–420) identified this 'Gospel according to the Hebrews' with one which he found in Syria, called the Gospel of the Nazarenes, and which he mistakenly thought at first was the Hebrew (or Aramaic) original of Matthew. It is possible that he was also mistaken in identifying it with the Gospel according to the Hebrews; the Nazarene Gospel found by Jerome (and translated by him into Greek and Latin) may simply have been an Aramaic translation of the canonical Greek Matthew. In any case, the Gospel according to the Hebrews and the Gospel of the Nazarenes[1] both had some relation to Matthew, and they are to be distinguished from the multitude of apocryphal Gospels which were also current in those days, and which have no bearing on our present historical study. These, like several books of apocryphal 'Acts', and similar writings, are almost entirely pure romances. One of the books of apocryphal Acts, however, the 'Acts of Paul', while admittedly a romance of the second century,[2] is interesting because of a pen-portrait of Paul which it contains, and which, because of its vigorous and unconventional character, was thought by Sir William Ramsay to embody a tradition of the apostle's appearance preserved in Asia Minor. Paul is described as 'a man small in size, with meeting eyebrows, with a rather large nose, baldheaded, bow-legged, strongly built, full of grace, for at times he looked like a man, and at times he had the face of an angel'.

---

[1] The existing fragments of both are translated in *The Apocryphal New Testament*, by M. R. James, pp. 1 ff.

[2] See M. R. James, *The Apocryphal New Testament*, pp. 270 ff.; W. M. Ramsay, *The Church in the Roman Empire* (1893), pp. 31 ff., 375 ff.

CHAPTER 4

THE GOSPELS

1. *The Synoptic Gospels*

WE now come to a more detailed examination of the Gospels. We have already indicated some of the evidence for their date and early attestation; we must now see what can be said about their origin and trustworthiness. The study of Gospel origins has been pursued with unflagging eagerness almost from the beginning of Christianity itself. Early in the second century we find Papias, bishop of Hierapolis in Asia Minor, gathering information on this and kindred subjects from Christians of an earlier generation than his own, men who had conversed with the apostles themselves. About AD 130–140 Papias wrote a work in five books (now lost except for a few fragments quoted by other writers), entitled *An Exposition of the Oracles of the Lord,* in the preface to which he says :

'But I will not hesitate to set down for you alongside my interpretations all that I ever learned well from the elders and remembered well, guaranteeing their truth. For I did not, like the majority, rejoice in those who say most, but in those who teach the truth; nor in those who record the commandments of others, but in those who relate the commandments given by the Lord to faith, and proceeding from Him who is the truth. Also, if ever a person came my way who had been a companion of the elders, I would inquire about the sayings of the elders—what was said by Andrew, or by Peter, or by Philip, or by Thomas or James, or by John or Matthew or any other of the Lord's disciples; and what things Aristion and the elder John, the disciples of the Lord, say. For I did not suppose that what I could get from books was of such great value to me as the utterances of a living and abiding voice.'[1]

Among the many things he learned from these elders and their associates was some information about the origins of the Gospels, which we shall look at shortly.

[1] Quoted by Eusebius, *Hist. Eccl.* iii. 39.

And from his days to our own men have pursued much the same quest, attempting not only to find out as much as possible from external and internal evidence about the writing of the Gospels, but trying also to get behind them to find out what they can about the sources which may lie behind the Gospels as they have come down to us. Of the fascination of this study, 'Source Criticism' as it is called, there can be no doubt. But the quest for Gospel sources and their hypothetical reconstruction may prove so engrossing that the student is apt to forget that the actual Gospels which have come down to us as literary units from the first century are necessarily more important than the putative documents which may be divined as their sources, if only because the latter have disappeared, if they ever existed, while the former have remained to our own day. And we must also remember that Source Criticism, interesting as it is, must necessarily lead to much less assured results than Textual Criticism, because it has to admit a much larger speculative element.

But provided that we bear in mind the limitations of this kind of literary criticism, there is considerable value in an inquiry into the sources of our Gospels. If the dates suggested for their composition in an earlier chapter are anything like correct, then no very long space of time separated the recording of the evangelic events from the events themselves. If, however, it can be shown with reasonable probability that these records themselves depend in whole or in part on still earlier documents, then the case for the trustworthiness of the gospel narrative is all the stronger.

Certain conclusions may be reached by a comparative study of the Gospels themselves. We are not long before we see that the Gospels fall naturally into two groups, the first three on one side, and the fourth Gospel by itself on the other. We shall revert to the problem of the fourth Gospel later, but for the present we must look at the other three, which are called the 'Synoptic' Gospels because they lend themselves to a synoptic arrangement, a form in which the three may be studied together.[1] It

[1] The first person to call them the Synoptic Gospels appears to have been the textual scholar J. J. Griesbach, in 1774.

requires no very detailed study to discover that these three have a considerable amount of material in common. We find, for example, that the substance of 606 out of the 661 verses of Mark appears in Matthew, and that some 350 of Mark's verses reappear with little material change in Luke. Or, to put it another way, out of the 1,068 verses of Matthew, about 500 contain material also found in Mark; of the 1,149 verses of Luke, about 350 are paralleled in Mark. Altogether, there are only 31 verses in Mark which have no parallel either in Matthew or Luke.

When we compare Matthew and Luke by themselves, we find that these two have about 250 verses containing common material not paralleled in Mark. This common material is cast in language which is sometimes practically identical in Matthew and Luke, and sometimes shows considerable divergence. We are then left with some 300 verses in Matthew containing narratives and discourses peculiar to that Gospel, and about 550 verses in Luke containing matter not found in the other Gospels.

These are facts which are easily ascertained; speculation enters when we try to explain them. Sometimes the material common to two or more of the Synoptists is so verbally identical that the identity can hardly be accidental. In this country the explanation commonly given last century was that the identity or similarity of language was due to the fact that the evangelists reproduced the language of the primitive oral gospel which was proclaimed in the early days of the Church. This is the view put forward, for example, in Alford's *Greek Testament* and in Westcott's *Introduction to the Study of the Gospels*. This theory later fell into disfavour, as it was realized that many of the phenomena could be more adequately explained by postulating documentary sources; but there was and is a great deal to be said for it, and it has reappeared in our own day in a somewhat different form in the approach known as Form Criticism.

Form Criticism aims at recovering the oral 'forms' or 'patterns' or 'moulds' in which the apostolic preaching and teaching were originally cast, even before the circulation of such documentary sources as may lie behind our Gospels. This method of approach has become popular since 1918, and its value has been exaggerated in some quarters, but one or two conclusions of importance emerge from it. One is that the hypothesis of documentary sources by itself is as inadequate to account for all the facts as was the 'oral theory' in the form propounded by Alford and Westcott; indeed, much of the recent popularity of Form Criticism may be due to dissatisfaction with the meagre results of a century's diligent pursuit of Source Criticism.

Another important point which is emphasized by Form Criticism is the universal tendency in ancient times to stereotype the 'forms' in which religious preaching and teaching were cast. This tendency can be widely traced in the ancient Gentile and Jewish world, and it is also manifest in our gospel material. In the days of the apostles there was a largely stereotyped preaching of the deeds and words of Jesus, originally in Aramaic but soon in Greek as well; and this preaching or oral tradition lies behind our Synoptic Gospels and their documentary sources.

We do not like stereotyped oral or literary styles; we prefer variety. But there are occasions on which a stereotyped style is insisted upon even in modern life. When, for example, a police officer gives evidence in court, he does not adorn his narrative with the graces of oratory, but adheres as closely as he can to a prescribed and stereotyped 'form'. The object of this is that the evidence he gives may conform as closely as possible to the actual course of events which he describes. What his narrative lacks in artistic finish, it gains in accuracy. The stereotyped style of many of the Gospel narratives and discourses serves the same end; it is a guarantee of their substantial accuracy. It frequently happens that, because of this preservation of a definite 'form', the reports of similar incidents or similar sayings will be given in much the same language and constructed on much the same framework. But we must not infer from this similarity of language and framework that two similar narratives are duplicate accounts of one and the same event, or that two similar parables (e.g. the wedding feast of Matthew xxii. 2 ff. and the great supper of Luke xiv. 16 ff.) are necessarily variant versions of one and the same parable, any more than we should conclude that, because a police officer describes two street accidents in almost identical language, he is really giving two variant accounts of one and the same street accident.

But perhaps the most important result to which Form Criticism points is that, no matter how far back we may press our researches into the roots of the gospel story, no matter how we classify the gospel material, we never arrive at a non-supernatural Jesus. The classification of our gospel material according to 'form' is by no means the most convenient or illuminating classification, but it adds a new method of grouping the material to others already known, and we are thus able to see that this fresh classification yields the same result as the others, the classifications, *e.g.*, by source or by subject-matter. All parts of the gospel record are shown by these various groupings to be pervaded by a consistent picture of Jesus as the Messiah, the Son of God; all agree in emphasizing the messianic significance of all that He said and did, and we can find no alternative picture, no matter how thoroughly we scrutinize and analyse successive strata of the Gospels. Thus Form Criticism has added its contribution to the overthrow of the hope once fondly held, that by getting back to the most primitive stage of gospel tradition we might recover a purely human Jesus, who simply taught the Fatherhood of God and the brotherhood of man.

The Gospel of Mark, because it was shorter than the others, and contained little that could not be found in them, was unduly neglected in ancient times. Augustine, for example, says that Mark seems to have followed Matthew 'as his lackey and abbreviator, so to speak'.[1] But anyone who studies a synopsis of the Gospels where the common material is arranged in parallel columns will see that for the most part it is Matthew and not Mark who abridges. Mark, of course, omits more than

[1] *De Consensu Evangelistarum*, i. 4.

half the material which appears in Matthew; but for the material which they have in common Mark is usually fuller than Matthew. Closer study of the linguistic and literary details of the Gospels in more recent times has led many scholars to the conclusion that Mark was actually the oldest of our Synoptic Gospels in their final form, and that it was a source of both Matthew and Luke. This 'Markan hypothesis',[1] as it is called, was adumbrated in the eighteenth century, but was first set on a stable basis by Carl Lachmann in 1835, when he showed that the common order of the three Synoptists is the order of Mark, since Mark and Matthew sometimes agree in order against Luke, and Mark and Luke still more frequently against Matthew, while Matthew and Luke never agree in order against Mark. Mark thus seems in this respect to be the norm from which the other two occasionally deviate. To this must be added the fact that most of the Markan subject-matter reappears in Matthew and Luke, with a considerable part of the actual language of Mark preserved, and that on grounds of literary criticism the differences in the presentation of common material between Mark on the one hand and Matthew and Luke on the other seem to be more easily accounted for by the priority of Mark than by the priority of Matthew or Luke. But while the Markan hypothesis is still the regnant hypothesis, it has been assailed by writers of great scholarship and ability. Thus the great German scholar Theodor von Zahn held that Matthew first composed his Gospel in Aramaic, that our Greek Mark was then composed in partial dependence on the Aramaic Matthew, and that the Aramaic Matthew was then turned into Greek with the aid of the Greek Mark.[2] Less complicated than Zahn's account is the view expressed by the Roman Catholic writers Dom John Chapman, *Matthew, Mark and Luke* (1937), and Dom B. C. Butler, *The Originality of St.*

[1] Here the term 'Markan hypothesis' is used solely in a literary sense, indicating the dependence of the two other Synoptists on Mark. The term has also been used of the view that only Mark's account of the ministry of Jesus has historical value — a view to which this book by no means subscribes.

[2] *Introduction to the New Testament* (1909), ii, p. 601.

Matthew's Gospel (1951), which turns the Markan hypothesis on its head and argues for the dependence of the
Greek Mark and Luke on the Greek Matthew.

The strength of the Markan hypothesis cannot be
conveyed in a sentence or two; the evidence is cumulative, and can best be appreciated by studying a good
synopsis (preferably Greek, but much of the evidence is
apparent even in an up-to-date English translation),
where the three Gospels have their parallel passages
arranged alongside each other in a form free from
prejudice in favour of any one hypothesis. Along with
such a synopsis, Greek students should examine the
linguistic data as marshalled by Sir John Hawkins in his
Horæ Synopticæ (2nd edition, 1909).

It is not so surprising as might at first appear to find
Mark, or something very like it, used as a source by the
other two Synoptists, when we consider what Mark
really is. Eusebius, in his *Ecclesiastical History* (iii. 39),
preserves for us a few sentences in which Papias tells us
the account of the origin of this Gospel which he
received from one whom he refers to as 'the Elder' :

> 'Mark, having been the interpreter of Peter, wrote down
> accurately all that he [Peter] mentioned, whether sayings or
> doings of Christ; not, however, in order. For he was neither
> a hearer nor a companion of the Lord; but afterwards, as I
> said, he accompanied Peter, who adapted his teachings as
> necessity required, not as though he were making a com-
> pilation of the sayings of the Lord. So then Mark made no
> mistake, writing down in this way some things as he [Peter]
> mentioned them; for he paid attention to this one thing, not
> to omit anything that he had heard, nor to include any false
> statement among them.'

This account has received illumination from a new
angle of recent years. Some Form Critics, attempting to
get behind the second Gospel, have envisaged it as consisting simply of independent stories and sayings which
had been transmitted orally in the primitive Church,
joined together by a sort of editorial cement in the form
of generalizing summaries which have no historical
value. But an examination of these 'generalizing summaries' reveals that, far from being editorial inventions,

they may be put together to form a consecutive outline
of the gospel narrative.[1] Now, in some of the early
summaries of the Christian preaching or 'Kerygma' in
Acts, we find similar outlines or partial outlines of the
gospel story.[2] These outlines in the Acts and Epistles
cover the period from the preaching of John the Baptist
to the resurrection of Christ, with more detailed
emphasis on the passion story. But this is exactly the
scope of the second Gospel, where, however, the outline
is filled in with illustrative incidents in the life of Christ
such as would naturally be used in preaching. It appears,
then, that Mark is, generally speaking, a statement of
the gospel story as it was related in the earliest days of
the Church, and, in view of Papias' description of Mark
as Peter's interpreter, it is noteworthy that Peter is the
chief preacher of the gospel in the early chapters of Acts.

Further confirmation of the Petrine authority behind
Mark was supplied in a series of acute linguistic studies
by C. H. Turner, entitled 'Marcan Usage', in the
Journal of Theological Studies for 1924 and 1925, showing, among other things, how Mark's use of pronouns
in narratives involving Peter seems time after time to
reflect a reminiscence by that apostle in the first person.
The reader can receive from such passages 'a vivid
impression of the testimony that lies behind the Gospel :
thus in i. 29, "we came into our house with James and
John : and my wife's mother was ill in bed with a fever,
and at once we tell him about her" '.[3]

There is, to be sure, much more in Mark's Gospel
than Peter's account of the ministry of Jesus. Mark
probably includes some reminiscences of his own. He
was in all probability the young man who had a narrow

[1] See especially C. H. Dodd, 'The Framework of the Gospel
Narrative', *Expository Times* xliii (1931-32), pp. 396 ff.

[2] *E.g.* Acts ii. 14 ff., iii. 12 ff., iv. 10 ff., v. 30 ff., x. 36 ff., xiii. 16 ff.;
cf. 1 Cor. xv. 3 ff.

[3] C. H. Turner, *The Gospel According to St. Mark*, in *A New Commentary on Holy Scripture* (S.P.C.K., 1928), Part III, p. 48. On p. 54
he lists the following passages in which 'Mark's third person plural
may be reasonably understood as representing a first person plural
of Peter's discourses': Mk. i. 21, 29, v. 1, 38, vi. 53, 54, viii. 22,
ix. 14, 30, 33, x. 32, 46, xi. 1, 12, 15, 20, 27, xiv. 18, 22, 26, 32.

escape when Jesus was arrested (Mk. xiv. 51 f.), and for some of the details of the passion narrative he may have drawn upon his own recollection of what he had seen on that occasion. There is a tradition that his parents' house (*cf.* Acts xii. 12) was the one in which the Last Supper was held.

The view that Mark underlies the other Synoptic Gospels is not so very different in essence from the older view that the common element in the three is the oral preaching current in the early Church; Mark is, by and large, that oral preaching written down. But the form in which the oral preaching underlies Matthew and Luke is the form given to it by Mark, who not only acted as Peter's interpreter (presumably translating Peter's Galilæan Aramaic into Greek), but incorporated in his Gospel the substance of the preaching as he heard it from Peter's lips. There is no lack of evidence in his Gospel that much of the material originally existed in Aramaic; his Greek in places preserves the Aramaic idiom quite unmistakably.

Mark's Gospel appears to have been written in the first instance for the Christian community of Rome, in the middle sixties of the first century, but it quickly enjoyed a very wide circulation throughout the Church.

The gospel as preached in those early days emphasized what Jesus *did* rather than what He *said*. The proclamation which led to the conversion of Jews and Gentiles was the good news that by His death and triumph He had procured remission of sins and opened the kingdom of heaven to all believers. But when they became Christians they had much more to learn, and in particular the teaching of Jesus. Now it is striking that the greater part of the non-Markan material common to Matthew and Luke consists of sayings of Jesus. This has led to the conjecture of another early document on which both Matthew and Luke drew for their common non-Markan material, the document usually referred to as 'Q', and envisaged as a collection of sayings of Jesus.[1] Whatever

[1] This postulated document was called Q independently, but almost simultaneously, by two scholars at the beginning of this century. In Germany Julius Wellhausen called it Q because that is

may be the truth about such a document, it will be convenient to use 'Q' as a symbol denoting this non-Markan material common to Matthew and Luke. There is evidence in the Greek of this 'Q' material that it has been translated from Aramaic, and possibly from an Aramaic document, not merely from an Aramaic oral tradition. Aramaic is known to have been the common language of Palestine, and especially of Galilee, in the time of Christ, and was in all probability the language which He and His apostles habitually spoke. The New Testament writers usually call it 'Hebrew', thus not distinguishing in name between it and its sister language in which most of the Old Testament was written. Now, we have evidence of an early Aramaic document in another fragment of Papias :[1]

'Matthew compiled the Logia in the "Hebrew" speech [*i.e.* Aramaic], and every one translated them as best he could.'

Various suggestions have been made as to the meaning of this term 'Logia', which literally means 'oracles'; but the most probable explanation is that it refers to a collection of our Lord's sayings. It is used in the New Testament of the oracles communicated through the Old Testament prophets, and Jesus was regarded by His followers as 'a prophet mighty in deed and word before God and all the people'.[2] Now, when an attempt is made to isolate the document underlying the 'Q' material in Matthew and Luke, it appears to have been constructed very much on the lines of one of the prophetical books of the Old Testament. These books commonly contain an account of the prophet's call to his distinctive ministry, with a record of his oracles set in a narrative framework, but no mention of the prophet's death. So this document, when reconstructed on the evidence provided by Matthew and Luke's Gospels, is seen to begin

the initial letter of German *Quelle*, meaning 'source'; in Cambridge J. Armitage Robinson, who designated the Markan source of the Synoptic material P (the initial of Peter, whose authority he believed to underlie Mark's Gospel), found it most natural to designate this second source by the following letter Q.

[1] Also preserved in Eusebius, *H.E.* iii. 39.   [2] Lk. xxiv. 19.

with an account of Jesus' baptism by John and His temptation in the wilderness, which formed the prelude to His Galilæan ministry, followed by groups of His sayings set in a minimum of narrative framework, but it evidently did not tell the story of His passion. His teaching is set forth in four main groupings, which may be entitled : (*a*) Jesus and John the Baptist; (*b*) Jesus and His disciples; (*c*) Jesus and His opponents; (*d*) Jesus and the future.[1]

It is difficult to avoid the conclusion that Papias was referring to just such a work as this when he said that Matthew compiled the Logia. His further statement, that the Logia were compiled in the 'Hebrew speech', accords with the internal evidence that an Aramaic substratum underlies the 'Q' material in Matthew and Luke. And when he adds that every man translated these Logia as best he could, this suggests that several Greek versions of them were current, which partly explains some of the differences in the sayings of Jesus common to the first and third Gospels; for in many places where the Greek of these Gospels differs, it can be shown that one and the same Aramaic original underlies the variant Greek renderings.

Another interesting fact which comes to light when we try to reconstruct the original Aramaic in which our Lord's sayings in all the Gospels were spoken is that very many of these sayings exhibit poetical features. Even in a translation we can see how full they are of parallelism, which is so constant a mark of Old Testament poetry. When they are turned into Aramaic, however, they are seen to be marked by regular poetical rhythm, and even, at times, rhyme. This has been demonstrated in particular by the late Professor C. F. Burney in *The Poetry of our Lord* (1925). A discourse that follows a recognizable pattern is more easily memorized, and if Jesus wished His teaching to be memorized His use of poetry is easily explained. Besides, Jesus was recognized by His contemporaries as a prophet, and prophets in Old Testament days were accustomed to utter their oracles in poetical form. Where this form has been preserved, we

[1] *Cf.* T. W. Manson, *The Sayings of Jesus* (1949), pp. 15-26.

have a further assurance that His teaching has been handed down to us as it was originally given.

So, just as we have found reason to see the authority of contemporary evidence behind the gospel narrative as preserved by Mark, the sayings of our Lord appear to be supported by similar trustworthy authority. But, in addition to the discourses in Matthew which have some parallel in Luke, there are others occurring in the first Gospel only, which may conveniently be denoted by the letter 'M'. These 'M' sayings have been envisaged as coming from another collection of the sayings of Jesus, largely parallel to the collection represented by 'Q', but compiled and preserved in the conservative Jewish–Christian community of Jerusalem, whereas the 'Q' material more probably served the requirements of the Hellenistic Christians who left Jerusalem after Stephen's death to spread the gospel and plant churches in the provinces adjoining Palestine, and notably in Syrian Antioch.

If we are right in naming the Matthæan Logia as the source from which the 'Q' material was drawn, this compilation must have taken shape at an early point in primitive Christian history. Certainly it would be most helpful for new converts, and especially Gentile converts, to have such a compendium of the teaching of Jesus. It may well have been in existence by AD 50. Some scholars have suggested that even Mark shows some traces of it in his Gospel, but this is uncertain.

The Gospel of Matthew seems to have appeared in the neighbourhood of Syrian Antioch some time after AD 70. It represents the substance of the apostolic preaching as recorded by Mark, expanded by the incorporation of other narrative material, and combined with a Greek version of the Matthæan Logia together with sayings of Jesus derived from other quarters. All this material has been arranged so as to serve the purpose of a manual for teaching and administration within the Church.[1] The sayings of Jesus are arranged so as to form five great discourses, dealing respectively with (*a*) the law of the kingdom of God (chapters v to vii), (*b*) the preaching of

[1] *Cf.* K. Stendahl, *The School of St. Matthew* (1968).

the kingdom (x. 5-42), (*c*) the growth of the kingdom (xiii. 3-52), (*d*) the fellowship of the kingdom (chapter xviii), and (*e*) the consummation of the kingdom (chapters xxiv-xxv). The narrative of the ministry of Jesus is so arranged that each section leads on naturally to the discourse which follows it. The whole is prefaced by a prologue describing the nativity of the King (chapters i-ii) and concluded by an epilogue relating the passion and triumph of the King (chapters xxvi-xxviii).

The fivefold structure of this Gospel is probably modelled on the fivefold structure of the Old Testament law; it is presented as the Christian *Torah* (which means 'direction' or 'instruction' rather than 'law' in the more restricted sense). The Evangelist is also at pains to show how the story of Jesus represents the fulfilment of the Old Testament Scriptures, and in places he even implies that the experiences of Jesus recapitulate the experiences of the people of Israel in Old Testament times. Thus, just as the children of Israel went down into Egypt in their national infancy and came out of it at the Exodus, so Jesus in His infancy must also go down to Egypt and come out of it, that the words spoken of them in Hosea xi. 1 might be fulfilled in His experience, too : 'Out of Egypt have I called my son' (Mt. ii. 15).

While some of the sayings of Jesus found in Luke are almost verbally identical with their Matthæan counterparts (*cf.* Lk. x. 21 f. with Mt. xi. 25-27), and others are reasonably similar, some show considerable differences, and it is unnecessary to suppose that for these last the first and third evangelists depended on one and the same documentary source. It is unlikely, for example, that the Matthæan and Lucan versions of the Beatitudes are drawn from one document (*cf.* Mt. v. 3 ff. with Lk. vi. 20 ff.). We have Luke's own statement that *many* had undertaken to draw up a narrative of the gospel history (Lk. i. 1), and it is unnecessarily narrowing the field to suppose that all the non-Markan material common in one form or another to Matthew and Luke must have been derived from one written source. To all appearances Luke was acquainted at a fairly early date with the Matthæan Logia, evidently in one or more of its

Greek versions. But he had other sources of information, and to them in particular he was indebted for those narratives and parables which give his Gospel its special charm and beauty. To this material peculiar to Luke we may conveniently assign the symbol 'L'.

Early tradition asserts that Luke was a native of Antioch.[1] If so, he had opportunities of learning many things from the founders of the Antiochene church, the first Gentile church (Acts xi. 19 ff.); he may even have met Peter, who once paid a visit there (Gal. ii. 11 ff.). He shows a special interest in the Herod family : was this due to his acquaintance with Manaen, foster-brother of Herod Antipas and one of the teachers in the church of Antioch (Acts xiii. 1)? Then he must have learned much from Paul. Though Paul had not been a follower of Jesus before the crucifixion, yet he must have made it his business after his conversion to learn as much about Him as he could (see chapter vi). What did Peter and Paul talk about during the fortnight they spent together in Jerusalem about AD 35 (Gal. i. 18)? As Professor Dodd puts it, 'we may presume they did not spend all the time talking about the weather.'[2] It was a golden opportunity for Paul to learn the details of the story of Jesus from one whose knowledge of that story was unsurpassed.

Again, Luke seems to have spent two years in or near Palestine during Paul's last visit to Jerusalem and detention in Cæsarea (cf. Acts xxiv. 27). These years afforded him unique opportunities of increasing his knowledge of the story of Jesus and of the early Church. On one occasion at least, he is known to have met James, the brother of Jesus; and he may have seized other opportunities of making the acquaintance of members of the holy family. Some of his special material reflects an oral Aramaic tradition, which Luke received from various Palestinian informants, while other parts of it were evidently derived from Christian Hellenists. In particular, there is reason to believe that much of the information which Luke used for the third Gospel and Acts was

[1] See p. 80.
   The Apostolic Preaching and its Developments (1936), p. 26.

derived from Philip and his family in Cæsarea (*cf.* Acts xxi. 8 f.).[1] Eusebius[2] tells us on the authority of Papias and other early writers that at a later date Philip's four prophetic daughters were famed in the Church as authorities for the history of its earliest days.

The account of the nativities of John the Baptist and Jesus in the first two chapters of the Gospel has been described as the most archaic passage in the New Testament; it breathes the atmosphere of a humble and holy Palestinian community which cherished ardent hopes of the early fulfilment of God's ancient promises to His people Israel, and saw in the birth of these two children a sign that their hopes were about to be realized. To this community belonged Mary and Joseph, with the parents of John the Baptist, and Simeon and Anna, who greeted the presentation of the infant Christ in the temple at Jerusalem, and later on Joseph of Arimathaea, 'who was looking for the kingdom of God' (Lk. xxiii. 51).

After Paul's two years of detention in Cæsarea, Luke went with him to Rome, and there we find him in Paul's company along with Mark about the year 60 (Col. iv. 10, 14; Phm. 24). His contact with Mark there is sufficient to account for his evident indebtedness to Mark's narrative. This summary of the way in which the third Gospel may have been built up is based on biblical evidence, and it accords very well with the internal data, evaluated by literary criticism which suggests that Luke first enlarged his version of the Matthæan Logia by adding the information he acquired from various sources, especially in Palestine. This first draft, 'Q' + 'L', has been called 'Proto-Luke',[3] though there is no evidence that it was ever published separately. It was subsequently amplified by the insertion at appropriate points of blocks of material derived from Mark, especially where the Markan material did not overlap the material

---

[1] *Cf.* A. Harnack, *Luke the Physician* (1907), pp. 153 ff.

[2] *Hist. Eccl.* iii. 31, 39.

[3] *Cf.* B. H. Streeter, *The Four Gospels* (1924), pp. 199 ff.; V. Taylor, *Behind the Third Gospel* (1926); *The Passion Narrative of St. Luke* (1972).

already collected, and thus our third Gospel was produced. Luke tells us in the preface to his Gospel that he had followed the whole course of events accurately from the beginning, and he evidently did this by having recourse to the best authorities he could find, and then arranging his material after the manner of a serious historian.[1]

Luke's arrival with Paul in Rome suggests itself as a fitting occasion for Luke's taking in hand to draw up his orderly and reliable account of Christian beginnings. If the official and cultured classes of Rome knew anything of Christianity before, they probably dismissed it as a disreputable eastern cult; but the presence in the city of a Roman citizen, who had appealed to Caesar for a fair hearing in a case which involved the whole question of the character and aims of Christianity, made it necessary for some members of these classes to examine Christianity seriously. The 'most excellent Theophilus', to whom Luke dedicated his twofold history, was possibly one of those who were charged with investigating the situation, and such a work as Luke's, even in a preliminary draft, would have been an invaluable document in the case.

We must never fall into the error of thinking that when we have come to a conclusion about the sources of a literary work we have learned all that needs to be known about it. Source Criticism is merely a preliminary piece of spade-work. Who would think that we have said all that is to be said about one of Shakespeare's historical plays when we have discovered what its sources were? So also, whatever their sources were, the Gospels are there before our eyes, each an individual literary work with its own characteristic viewpoint, which has in large measure controlled the choice and presentation of the subject-matter. In attempting to discover how they were composed, we must beware of regarding them as scissors-and-paste compilations.

Each of them was written in the first instance for a definite constituency, with the object of presenting Jesus of Nazareth as Son of God and Saviour. Mark entitles

[1] See further pp. 80 ff. below.

his work 'the beginning of the good news of Jesus the Messiah, the Son of God', and towards the end we find a Roman centurion confessing at the foot of the cross, 'Truly this man was the Son of God' (Mk. xv. 39). We may imagine how effective this testimony must have been in Rome, where this Gospel was first published. Luke, the Gentile physician, inheriting the traditions of Greek historical writing, composes his work after diligent research in order that his readers may know the secure basis of the account of Christian origins which they have received, and withal infuses into it such a spirit of broad human sympathy that many have been constrained to pronounce his Gospel, with Ernest Renan, 'the most beautiful book in the world'. Matthew's Gospel occupies by right its place at the head of the New Testament canon; what other book could so fittingly form the link between the Old and New Testaments as that which proclaims itself, in language reminiscent of the first book of the Old Testament canon, 'The book of the generation of Jesus the Messiah, the Son of David, the Son of Abraham'? Although it has been called the most Jewish of the Gospels, yet it does not encourage national particularism or religious exclusiveness, for this is the Gospel which ends with the rejected but vindicated King of Israel's commission to His servants: 'Go and make disciples of all the nations' (Mt. xxviii. 19).

The evidence indicates that the written sources of our Synoptic Gospels are not later than *c.* AD 60; some of them have even been traced back to notes taken of our Lord's teaching while His words were actually being uttered. The oral sources go back to the very beginning of Christian history. We are, in fact, practically all the way through in touch with the evidence of eyewitnesses. The earliest preachers of the gospel knew the value of this first-hand testimony, and appealed to it time and again. 'We are witnesses of these things,' was their constant and confident assertion. And it can have been by no means so easy as some writers seem to think to invent words and deeds of Jesus in those early years, when so many of His disciples were about, who could remember

what had and had not happened. Indeed, the evidence
is that the early Christians were careful to distinguish
between sayings of Jesus and their own inferences or
judgments. Paul, for example, when discussing the vexed
questions of marriage and divorce in 1 Corinthians vii,
is careful to make this distinction between his own advice
on the subject and the Lord's decisive ruling : 'I, not the
Lord,' and again, 'Not I, but the Lord.'

And it was not only friendly eyewitnesses that the
early preachers had to reckon with; there were others
less well disposed who were also conversant with the
main facts of the ministry and death of Jesus. The disciples could not afford to risk inaccuracies (not to speak
of wilful manipulation of the facts), which would at once
be exposed by those who would be only too glad to do
so. On the contrary, one of the strong points in the
original apostolic preaching is the confident appeal to
the knowledge of the hearers; they not only said, 'We
are witnesses of these things,' but also, 'As you yourselves
also know' (Acts ii. 22). Had there been any tendency
to depart from the facts in any material respect, the
possible presence of hostile witnesses in the audience
would have served as a further corrective.

We have then in the Synoptic Gospels, the latest of
which was complete between forty and fifty years after
the death of Christ, material which took shape at a still
earlier time, some of it even before His death, and
which, besides being for the most part first-hand evidence, was transmitted along independent and trustworthy lines. The Gospels in which this material is
embodied agree in their presentation of the basic facts
of the Christian faith—a threefold cord not quickly
broken.

2. *The Fourth Gospel*

In his *Argument to the Gospel of John,* the great Re-
former John Calvin says : 'I am in the habit of saying
that this Gospel is the key which opens the door to the
understanding of the others.' His opinion has been
endorsed by Christian thinkers of many ages, who have
found in this Gospel depths of spiritual truth unreached

in any other New Testament writing. To the question whether the discourses in this Gospel are genuine words of Christ, not a few would reply that, if they are not, then a greater than Christ is here.

Yet, during the last hundred years especially, the fourth Gospel has been the centre of unending disputes. People talk about the enigma of the fourth Gospel, and what is confidently accepted by one side as an adequate solution is with equal confidence rejected by another side as untenable. This is not the place to undertake a fresh solution; it must suffice to mention some of the most important facts bearing on this Gospel's historicity.

The claim of the Gospel itself is that it was written by an eyewitness. In the last chapter we read of a resurrection appearance of Jesus by the Sea of Galilee, at which seven disciples were present, including one who is called 'the disciple whom Jesus loved'. A note at the end of the chapter tells us : 'This is the disciple who testifies of these things and who wrote these things, and we know that his testimony is true' (Jn. xxi. 24). It is not quite clear who are the 'we' who thus add their testimony to the evangelist's veracity; they were probably the group of friends and disciples associated with him who were responsible for the editing and publication of his Gospel. This 'disciple whom Jesus loved' is mentioned also as one of the company at the Last Supper (xiii. 23), as being present at the crucifixion (xix. 26),[1] and as an eyewitness, in Peter's company, of the empty tomb on the resurrection morning (xx. 2 ff.). Do these passages give us any clue to his identity?

According to Mark xiv. 17,[2] when our Lord arrived at the upper room for the Last Supper, He was accompanied by the twelve apostles, who reclined at table

---

[1] It was to the care of the beloved disciple that our Lord on the cross committed His mother (Jn. xix. 26 f.). A comparison of Matthew xxvii. 56 and Mark xv. 40 with John xix. 25 suggests that Salome, the mother of James and John, was the sister of our Lord's mother; it was natural, therefore, that He should commit her to His cousin, who was at hand and who believed in Him, rather than to His brothers, who may not have been available at the time, and who in any case did not believe until He rose from the dead.

[2] *Cf.* Mt. xxvi. 20; Lk. xxii. 14.

with Him, and there is no suggestion in the Synoptic Gospels that anyone else was present with Him on that occasion. We conclude, therefore, that the 'beloved disciple' was one of the twelve. Now, of the twelve, there were three who were on occasion admitted to more intimate fellowship with the Master—Peter, James and John. It was these three, for example, whom He took to keep watch with Him during His vigil in Gethsemane after the Last Supper (Mk. xiv. 33). We should naturally expect that the beloved disciple would be one of the number. He was not Peter, from whom he is explicitly distinguished in xiii. 24, xx. 2 and xxi. 20. There remain the two sons of Zebedee, James and John, who were included in the seven of chapter xxi. But James was martyred not later than AD 44 (Acts xii. 2),[1] and therefore there was little likelihood that the saying should go abroad about him which went abroad about the beloved disciple, that he would not die. So we are left with John.

Now it is noteworthy that John is not mentioned by name in the fourth Gospel (nor yet is his brother James). It has also been pointed out that while the other evangelists refer to John the Baptist as John the Baptist, the fourth evangelist refers to him simply as John. An author will take care to distinguish two characters in his narrative who bear the same name; he will not be so careful to distinguish one of his characters from himself. The fourth evangelist himself distinguishes Judas Iscariot from Judas 'not Iscariot' (xiv. 22). It is significant, therefore, that he does not distinguish John the Baptist from John the apostle, of whom he must have known, though he does not mention him by name.

In general, the internal evidence reveals an author who was an eyewitness of the events he describes. It is interesting in this connection to quote the verdict of

[1] The theory that John also suffered martyrdom at an early date rests on the flimsiest foundation. Professor A. S. Peake's verdict was a sound one: 'The alleged martyrdom of the apostle John I firmly disbelieve. It has gained a credence amazing in view of the slender evidence on which it is built, which would have provoked derision if it had been adduced in favour of a conservative conclusion' (*Holborn Review*, June, 1928, p. 384).

Miss Dorothy Sayers, who approached the subject from the standpoint of a creative artist : 'It must be remembered that, of the four Evangels, St. John's is the only one that claims to be the direct report of an eyewitness. And to any one accustomed to the imaginative handling of documents, the internal evidence bears out this claim.'[1] Even the miraculous narratives in the Gospel exhibit this quality. Thus, for example, the late A. T. Olmstead, Professor of Ancient Oriental History in the University of Chicago, finds the story of the raising of Lazarus in chapter xi to have 'all the circumstantial detail of the convinced eyewitness'[2], while the narrative of the empty tomb in chapter xx is 'told by an undoubted eyewitness—full of life, and lacking any detail to which the sceptic might take justifiable objection'.[3]

The evangelist was evidently a Palestinian. Although he may have been far from his native land when he wrote his Gospel, his accurate knowledge of places and distances in Palestine, a knowledge which appears spontaneously and naturally, strongly suggests one who was born and brought up in that land, not one whose knowledge of the country was derived from pilgrim-visits. He knows Jerusalem well; he fixes the location of certain places in the city with the accuracy of one who must have been acquainted with it before its destruction in AD 70.

The author was also a Jew; he is thoroughly conversant with Jewish customs; he refers to their purification rites (ii. 6) and their manner of burial (xix. 40). Of their feasts, he mentions the Passover, the Feast of Tabernacles, and the Feast of Dedication, held in winter, together with the unnamed feast of v. 1 which was probably the Feast of the New Year.[4] He shows himself intimately acquainted with the Old Testament passages which the Palestinian Jewish lectionary prescribed for reading in synagogue at the festivals and other periods

[1] D. L. Sayers, *The Man Born to be King* (1943), p. 33. Her whole discussion on pp. 28 ff. is worthy of careful attention. *Cf.* also her remarks on this Gospel in *Unpopular Opinions* (1946), pp. 25 ff.

[2] *Jesus in the Light of History* (1942), p. 206.   [3] *Op. cit.*, p. 248.

[4] An unusual and fascinating discussion of this feast will be found in J. R. Harris, *Side-lights on New Testament Research* (1908), pp. 52 ff.

of the year.[1] He knows the Jewish law of evidence (viii. 17). He is familiar with the superior attitude of those who had received a rabbinical training towards those who had not enjoyed this advantage—'These people who do not know the Law are accursed' (vii. 49)—an attitude expressed even by the liberal Rabbi Hillel: 'No ignorant person is pious.'[2] He had been accused of the crass error of supposing that a high priest of the Jews held office for only a year; but when in his passion narrative he refers to Caiaphas as 'high priest that year' (xi. 49, 51, xviii. 13) he simply means that he was high priest in the fateful year of Jesus' crucifixion.

John's accurate knowledge of Jewish customs, beliefs, and methods of argument led a great rabbinical scholar, the late Israel Abrahams, to say: 'My own general impression, without asserting an early date for the Fourth Gospel, is that the Gospel enshrines a genuine tradition of an aspect of Jesus' teaching which has not found a place in the Synoptics.'[3] Abrahams also emphasized 'the cumulative strength of the arguments adduced by Jewish writers favourable to the authenticity of the discourses in the Fourth Gospel, especially in relation to the circumstances under which they are reported to have been spoken.'[4]

The internal evidence supports the claim that the author not only witnessed but understood the great events which he records. The external evidence for the Gospel is as strong as for the Synoptics. We have already mentioned the papyrus evidence which attests its early date. Ignatius, whose martyrdom took place about AD 115, was influenced by the distinctive teaching of this Gospel; and Polycarp, writing to the Philippian church shortly after Ignatius' martyrdom, quotes the First Epistle of John, which, in the opinion of Lightfoot, Westcott and others, accompanied the Gospel as a covering letter, and is in any case closely related to it.

---

[1] The pioneer work on this subject is A. E. Guilding, *The Fourth Gospel and Jewish Worship* (1959).
[2] *Pirqe Aboth* ii. 6.
[3] I. Abrahams, *Studies in Pharisaism and the Gospels*, i (1917), p. 12.
[4] In *Cambridge Biblical Essays*, ed. H. B. Swete (1909), p. 181.

The Gnostic Basilides (*c.* AD 130) cites John i. 9 as 'in the Gospels'. Justin Martyr (*c.* AD 150) quotes from the Nicodemus story of John iii. His disciple Tatian (*c.* AD 170) included the fourth Gospel in his *Diatessaron*. About the same time Melito, bishop of Sardis, shows dependence on this Gospel in his *Easter Homily*.

Apart from these early evidences of the existence of the fourth Gospel, we find in several second-century writers observations on its authorship. In the last quarter of that century Irenæus, who had connections with both Asia Minor and Gaul, Clement of Alexandria, Theophilus of Antioch, Tertullian of Carthage, and the Gnostic Heracleon in Italy, the earliest known commentator on the fourth Gospel, attest the generally held belief that the author was John.[1]

Of these witnesses the most important is Irenæus. 'John, the disciple of the Lord,' he says, 'the same who reclined upon His breast, himself also published his Gospel, when he was living in Ephesus in Asia.'[2] Elsewhere he refers to him as 'the apostle'.[3] Again, in his letter to Florinus,[4] Irenæus reminds him of their early days when they had sat at the feet of Polycarp, bishop of Smyrna (who was martyred in AD 156 when he had been a Christian for eighty-six years). Polycarp in his turn had been a disciple of John, and Irenæus and Florinus had often heard him speak of what John and other eyewitnesses told him about Christ.

Other evidence about the authorship of the Gospel is

---

[1] In the second century the only dissenting voices appear to be those of people who disliked the Logos ('Word') doctrine of the Prologue, and therefore denied the apostolic authorship, ascribing it to Cerinthus, a heretic who flourished at the end of the first century. Epiphanius calls these people *alogoi*, which meant not only that they rejected the Logos doctrine, but also that they were devoid of *logos* in the sense of 'reason'. The only person of consequence connected with them seems to have been the learned Gaius of Rome (*c.* AD 200), who was an orthodox churchman except for his rejection of the fourth Gospel and the Revelation. Apart from them, this Gospel appears to have been generally accepted in the second century by orthodox and heretics alike.

[2] *Adv. Haer.* iii. 1.

[3] *Ibid.* i. 9, etc.

[4] Quoted by Eusebius *Hist. Eccl.* v. 20.

found towards the end of the second century in the Muratorian Fragment and in the anti-Marcionite prologue to the fourth Gospel. The former document tells this strange story :

'John one of the disciples, wrote the fourth of the gospels. When his fellow-disciples and bishops urged him, he said: "Fast along with me for three days, and then let us relate to one another what shall be revealed to each." The same night it was revealed to Andrew, one of the apostles, that John should write down everything in his own name, and that they should all revise it.'

Andrew was certainly not alive at the time referred to. But the fragment may preserve a true tradition that several persons were concerned in the production of the Gospel, for we think of the men who append their testimonial to the evangelist's record in John xxi. 24 : 'we know that his witness is true.'

The other document, the anti-Marcionite prologue, which is much more important, runs as follows :

'The gospel of John was published and given to the churches by John when he was still in the body, as a man of Hierapolis, Papias by name, John's dear disciple, has related in his five Exegetical[1] books. He indeed wrote down the gospel correctly at John's dictation. But the heretic Marcion was thrust out by John, after being repudiated by him for his contrary sentiments. He had carried writings or letters to him from brethren who were in Pontus.'

The reference to Marcion is probably a confused reminiscence of an earlier statement that *Papias* had refused to countenance him.[2] Apart from that, the prologue contains the important evidence that Papias in his *Exposition of the Oracles of the Lord* (*c.* AD 130-140) stated that John dictated the fourth Gospel. This is therefore our earliest external evidence for the Johannine authorship of the Gospel. The statement that it was Papias who wrote down the Gospel at John's dicta-

[1] The Greek copy from which the extant Latin of this Prologue was translated had the scribal error *exoterikois* for *exegetikois*.

[2] This reference to Marcion is one of the starting-points for Dr. Robert Eisler's curious theory propounded in his *Enigma of the Fourth Gospel* (1938), according to which Marcion was John's amanuensis, and was dismissed by him when he was discovered to have made heretical interpolations in the Gospel as he copied it!

tion is unsupported and in any case improbable. Bishop Lightfoot made the very attractive suggestion that Papias wrote that the Gospel was 'delivered by John to the Churches, which *they* wrote down from his lips', but that he was wrongly taken to mean 'which *I* wrote down from his lips', since the Greek forms for 'I wrote' and 'they wrote' are identical in the imperfect tense (*apegraphon*) and very similar in the aorist (1st sing. *apegrapsa*; 3rd plur. *apegrapsan,* perhaps written *apegrapsā*).[1] Other explanations have been proposed. In a letter to *The Times* of 13 February 1936, Dr. F. L. Cross wrote : 'My own reading of the prologue, if I may set it down dogmatically, is that in its original form it asserted that the fourth gospel was written by John the elder at the dictation of John the apostle when the latter had reached a very great age.'

For this John the elder we must turn to the fragment of Papias quoted on p. 29, where two Johns seem to be distinguished, one being spoken of in the past tense, the other in the present. Some scholars, indeed, have held that Papias refers to only one John; the more natural reading of the fragment, however, indicates a reference to two.[2] Unfortunately, Papias is not the most lucid of writers, and his work survives only in fragments, so it is difficult to be sure of his meaning. It may well be that John the elder was a presbyter of Ephesus, and a disciple of John the apostle. There was a considerable migration of Palestinian Christians to the province of Asia in the third quarter of the first century; but John the apostle was the most distinguished of the migrants. (Philip and his daughters, who have been mentioned above, migrated at the same time.) But we need not metamorphose the obscure 'elder John' into such an unrecognized genius as he must have been if some theories of his activity are true. Some difficulties and inconsistencies in statements made by writers of the early Christian centuries may be

[1] J. B. Lightfoot, *Essays on 'Supernatural Religion'* (1889), p. 214.
[2] So eminently orthodox a scholar as S. P. Tregelles had no hesitation in finding two Johns in the passage (*New Testament Historic Evidence* [1851], p. 47). Cf. F. F. Bruce, *Men and Movements in the Primitive Church* (1979), pp. 133-136.

due to a confusion of the two Johns; but it is highly
unlikely that Irenæus was guilty of such a confusion,
and thought that his master Polycarp was speaking of
the apostle when in fact he was speaking of the elder.
If John the elder is to be distinguished from the apostle,
then one could easily envisage him as the copyist and
editor of the fourth Gospel (though the evidence for this
is rather slender), but probably not as the evangelist in
person.

Some scholars have argued that our Gospel of John
was translated from an Aramaic original. While this
thesis has been presented with great ability, the case
falls short of proof. The argument is strongest for the
discourses of Jesus. Thus, reviewing C. F. Burney's
Aramaic Origin of the Fourth Gospel (1922), Professor
G. R. Driver pointed out that Burney's most cogent
examples occurred in the *ipsissima verba* of our Lord
and other speakers.[1] But the Greek style of the Gospel
as a whole could well be that of someone who had a
good command of Greek but whose native language was
Aramaic.

The evidence thus far, whether internal or external,
might be thought to be in favour of the apostolicity of
the Gospel. What, then, are the difficulties? Little weight
can be attached to the objection that a simple fisherman
would not be likely to compose a work of such profound
thought. The author of the Pauline Epistles was a tent-
maker, despite his rabbinical training, for it was considered fitting that a Rabbi should earn his living by a
worldly occupation. John, the son of Zebedee, had no
rabbinical training, and therefore he and Peter were
considered 'unlearned and ignorant men'—'uneducated
laymen'—by the Sanhedrin (Acts iv. 13); but he had
been a disciple of no ordinary Teacher, and as he was
probably quite a young man at the time of the death of
Christ he had plenty of time and capacity for mental
and spiritual development. We remember how in England a tinker of Bedford showed no mean capacity for
spiritual literature.

[1] In *The Original Language of the Fourth Gospel*, reprinted from *The Jewish Guardian* for 5 and 12 January 1923.

The problem of the fourth Gospel presents itself most acutely when we compare it with the Synoptics. For one thing, it seems to diverge from them in matters of geography, chronology, and diction.

The main geographical divergence is that while the Synoptists tell almost exclusively of a Galilæan ministry, John places most of our Lord's activity in Jerusalem and Judæa. This is not a serious difficulty; John knows of His Galilæan ministry (*cf.* Jn. vii. 1), and the Synoptists implicitly confirm the Johannine account of a Jerusalem ministry. According to them, He is known by the owner of an ass in a village near Jerusalem (Mk. xi. 3-6), He is expected for the Passover by the proprietor of a room in Jerusalem (Mk. xiv. 12-16), and in His lament over Jerusalem He says : '*How often* would I have gathered your children together' (Mt. xxiii. 37; Lk. xiii. 34). John quite possibly knew the other Gospels, and for the most part does not overlap them, but rather supplements them.

The chronological differences are also easily disposed of. The Galilæan ministry described by the Synoptists lasted for about a year; but John takes us farther back to a southern ministry of Christ before the imprisonment of John the Baptist. The year of Galilæan ministry, recorded by the Synoptists, is to be fitted into the Johannine framework between John v and vii, ending with the Feast of Tabernacles of John vii. 2.[1] The activity of Jesus in the south of Palestine before His Galilæan ministry throws light on some episodes in the Synoptics. We read the Synoptic story of the call of Peter, Andrew, James and John with fresh understanding when we learn from John i. 37 ff. that they had met the Master before in the company of John the Baptist.

These earlier chapters of John's Gospel, dealing with a Judæan phase of Jesus' ministry which was concurrent with the later ministry of the Baptist, have received fresh illumination from the new knowledge about the community of Qumran, north-west of the Dead Sea, which we owe to the discovery and study of the Dead

[1] *Cf.* G. Ogg, *The Chronology of the Public Ministry of Jesus* (1940), the leading work on the subject.

Sea Scrolls and the excavation of Khirbet Qumran. The dispute about purification mentioned in a baptismal setting in John iii. 25 is the sort of dispute which must have been very common in the Jordan valley and the Dead Sea region at a time when many competing 'baptist' groups inhabited those parts. The disciples of John and the disciples of Jesus were not the only people engaged in baptizing there in those days. The members of the Qumran community had their own ceremonial washings, as had the members of other communities.

As for the events which John places after the Galilæan ministry, a careful comparison of his Gospel with the other three (and especially with Luke's) will show that the Synoptic narrative becomes more intelligible if we follow John in believing that the Galilæan ministry ended in autumn of AD 29, that Jesus then went to Jerusalem for the Feast of Tabernacles, that He stayed there until the Feast of Dedication in December (Jn. x. 22), that He then spent some months in retirement in the Jordan valley (Jn. x. 40), returning to Jerusalem about a week before the Passover of AD 30 (Jn. xii. 1).[1]

In fact, John's record, by its recurring mention of periodic festivals, provides a helpful chronological framework for the Synoptic narrative, which is lacking in chronological indications for the period between Jesus' baptism and His last visit to Jerusalem. Mark does mention that there was much 'green grass' around when the five thousand were fed (vi. 39); this accords well with the statement of John vi. 4 that this took place shortly before the Passover (of 17 April, AD 29). Indeed, several scholars who decline to accept as historical John's portrait of Christ are quite willing to accept his chronological framework. There is some difficulty in reconciling his chronology of Passion Week with the Synoptic data, but this difficulty might disappear if we were better acquainted with the conditions under which the Passover was celebrated at that time. There is considerable ground for believing that certain religious groups (including our Lord and His disciples) followed a differ-

[1] *Cf.* M. Goguel, *Life of Jesus* (1933), p. 400.

ent calendar from that by which the chief priests regulated the temple services. While the chief priests and those who followed their reckoning ate the Passover on Friday evening, when Jesus was already dead (Jn. xviii. 28, xix. 14), He and His disciples appear to have eaten it twenty-four hours earlier.[1]

As for differences in diction between this Gospel and the others, there is no doubt that the fourth evangelist has his own very distinctive style, which colours not only his own meditations and comments but the sayings of Jesus and of John the Baptist. This phenomenon has sometimes been described as his transposition of the gospel story into another key. We must remember, of course, that the sayings of Jesus and John, as this evangelist records them, are translations of an oral Aramaic original; and it is antecedently probable that a disciple who had penetrated so deeply into our Lord's mind should have been unconsciously influenced by His style, so that it coloured all that he wrote. Partly because of this, it is, at times, difficult to decide where the Master's words end and where the disciple's meditations begin.

The Synoptic Gospels themselves bear witness to the fact that Jesus sometimes spoke in the style which He regularly uses in John's Gospel. Part of the difference in style between His teaching in the Synoptic Gospels and in this Gospel may be due to the difference in environment. In the Synoptic Gospels He is conversing, for the most part, with the country people of Galilee; in the fourth Gospel he disputes with the religious leaders of Jerusalem or talks intimately to the inner circle of His disciples. We must not tie Him down to one style of speech. The same poetical patterns as appear in the Synoptic discourses recur in the Johannine discourses.[2] The Synoptists and John agree in ascribing to Him the characteristic asseveration 'Verily (literally, Amen), I tell

---

[1] Annie Jaubert, in *The Date of the Last Supper* (1965), argued that the Last Supper, according to the Qumran calendar, took place on the Tuesday evening, so that some sixty hours elapsed between Jesus' arrest and crucifixion. This interval is certainly too long.

[2] *Cf.* C. F. Burney, *The Poetry of our Lord* (1925).

you,' except that in John the 'Amen' is always repeated. And even in the Synoptists we come, now and again, on some thoroughly Johannine phraseology. In John our Lord frequently speaks of His Father as 'him who sent me'; the same phrase appears in Mark ix. 37 : 'Whosoever receives me, receives not me, but him who sent me' (*cf*. Mt. x. 40; Lk. ix. 48), almost the same words as we find in John xii. 44, xiii. 20. Still more striking is the passage in Matthew xi. 27 and Luke x. 22 : 'All things have been delivered to me by my Father; and no one knows the Son except the Father, nor does anyone know the Father except the Son and any to whom the Son is willing to reveal him'—an 'erratic block of Johannine rock', as it has been called.

It is worth mentioning here that striking affinities of thought and language have been recognized between this Gospel and the Qumran texts. These affinities must not be exaggerated; the Qumran literature comes nowhere near presenting us with such a figure as the Jesus of this Gospel. Yet the texts provide additional evidence for the basically Hebraic character of this Gospel. They appear especially in the phraseology which opposes light to darkness, truth to error, and so forth; and also in certain forms of messianic expectation which find expression both in the fourth Gospel and at Qumran.

We also meet quite remarkable similarities to the thought and language of the fourth Gospel in the Syriac collection of Christian hymns rather oddly entitled the *Odes of Solomon,* which belong to the end of the first or the early part of the second century.

But the most important question of all is that of the portrayal of Christ Himself. Does John present to us the same Christ as the Synoptists do? He is at one with them in viewing Jesus as Messiah and Son of God. If his purpose in writing the Gospel was that his readers might believe that Jesus was Messiah and Son of God, as he tells us (Jn. xx. 31), then we may recall that Mark introduces *his* record with very similar words : 'The beginning of the gospel of Jesus the Messiah, the Son of God' (Mk. i. 1). There is, in fact, no material difference in Christology between John and the three Synoptists. He does indeed view Jesus as the pre-existent Word of God, the Eternal Father's agent in creation, revelation and redemption; but he does not emphasize His deity at the expense of His humanity. Jesus grows tired on His journey through Samaria (Jn. iv. 6); He weeps at the grave of Lazarus (xi. 35); He thirsts upon the cross (xix. 28). Indeed, John is at pains to refute a current fancy that our Lord's humanity was only apparent and not real; that is why he insists so unambiguously that 'the Word became flesh' (Jn. i. 14) and affirms so solemnly, with the authority of an eyewitness, that there was nothing unreal about His death on the cross (xix. 30-35).

We do, indeed, get a different impression of the self-disclosure of Jesus in this Gospel from that given by the Synoptists. In them the fact that Jesus is the Messiah is first realized by the disciples towards the end of the Galilæan ministry, at Cæsarea Philippi, and Jesus gives them strict instructions to keep it to themselves; moreover, it is only then that He begins to speak about His forthcoming passion (Mk. viii. 27 ff.). In John His messianic dignity is recognized by others and acknowledged by Himself quite early in the record, while He speaks (in somewhat veiled language, to be sure) about the necessity for His death almost at the beginning of His ministry. The evangelist, of course, who had meditated for many years on the significance of the acts and words of Jesus, had learned to appreciate even the earliest stages of the ministry in the light of its consummation. Moreover, while Jesus might well refuse to blaze abroad His Messiahship in the revolutionary atmosphere of Galilee,[1] there were sections of the population in Jerusalem who had to be confronted more directly with His claims, although even there it was a matter of complaint only three or four months before His death that He would not tell them plainly whether He was the Messiah or not (Jn. x. 24).

The last survivor of those who were most closely

[1] *Cf.* C. E. Raven, *Jesus and the Gospel of Love* (1931), p. 216. Chapters vii and viii of Dr. Raven's book are worthy of careful study in relation to the problems of the fourth Gospel.

associated with Jesus during His ministry thought long and deeply about the meaning of all that he had seen and heard. Much that had once been obscure became clearer to his mind with the passage of time.

'What once were guessed as points, I now knew stars,
And named them in the Gospel I have writ.'[1]

In his old age he realized more than ever that, although the conditions of life in Palestine which had formed the setting for Jesus' ministry before AD 30 had passed away beyond recall, that ministry itself—indeed, the whole span of years that Jesus had spent on earth—was charged with eternal validity. In the life of Jesus all the truth of God which had ever been communicated to men was summed up and made perfect; in Him the eternal Word or self-expression of God had come home to the world in a real human life. But if this was so, the life and work of Jesus could have no merely local, national or temporary relevance. So, towards the end of the first century, he set himself to tell the gospel story in such a way that its abiding truth might be presented to men and women who were quite unfamiliar with the original setting of the saving events. The Hellenistic world of his old age required to be told the regenerating message in such a way that, whether Jews or Gentiles, they might be brought to faith in Jesus as the Messiah and Son of God, and thus receive eternal life through Him. Yet he would not yield to any temptation to restate Christianity in terms of contemporary thought in such a way as to rob it of its essential uniqueness. The gospel is eternally true, but it is the story of events which happened in history once for all; John does not divorce the story from its Palestinian context in order to bring out its universal application, and at the heart of his record the original apostolic preaching is faithfully preserved.[2]

Did he succeed in his aim? Whatever difficulties some scholars have felt, most readers of the Gospels in all ages have been unaware of any fundamental discrepancy

[1] Robert Browning, *A Death in the Desert.*
[2] This is well brought out by Professor C. H. Dodd in *The Interpretation of the Fourth Gospel* (1953), the most important work to appear in this field for a generation.

between the Christ who speaks and acts in the fourth Gospel and Him who speaks and acts in the Synoptics. Many have testified that John leads them into an even deeper and more intimate appreciation of the mind of Christ than do the other three. The members of the Christian Industrial League, an organization which carries on a gospel witness among the tough characters of Skidrow, in the heart of Chicago's 'Loop' area, say 'that in their work they have found that St. John's Gospel is the best for dealing with these tough, hard men. Its straight, unequivocal words about sin and salvation somehow go home and carry conviction to the most abandoned, while its direct invitation wins a response that nothing else does.'[1] Or we may listen to a testimony from a very different source, the late Archbishop William Temple, theologian, philosopher and statesman :

> 'The Synoptists may give us something more like the perfect photograph; St. John gives us the more perfect portrait . . . the mind of Jesus Himself was what the Fourth Gospel disclosed, but . . . the disciples were at first unable to enter into this, partly because of its novelty, and partly because of the associations attaching to the terminology in which it was necessary that the Lord should express Himself. Let the Synoptists repeat for us as closely as they can the very words He spoke; but let St. John tune our ears to hear them.'[2]

It is evident that John's aim has been realized, not only among Jewish and Gentile readers of the Hellenistic world at the end of the first century AD, but throughout successive generations to our own day. As he introduces us to Jesus as the perfect revealer of God, as love incarnate, as the embodiment of that life which has ever been the light of men, there are many to whom his record comes home with the self-authenticating testimony which characterizes eternal truth, as it constrains them to endorse the statement of those men who first gave the evangelist's words to the public : 'we know that his witness is true.'

[1] A. M. Chirgwin, *The Bible in World Evangelism* (1954), p. 113.
[2] *Readings in St. John's Gospel* (1940), pp. xvi, xxxii.

CHAPTER 5

THE GOSPEL MIRACLES

BEFORE we leave the Gospels, something ought to be said about the miracle-stories which are found in them. Anyone who attempts to answer the question which forms the title of this book must recognize that for many readers it is precisely these miracle-stories which are the chief difficulty in the way of accepting the New Testament documents as reliable.

To some extent it is true to say that the credibility of these stories is a matter of historical evidence. If they are related by authors who can be shown on other grounds to be trustworthy, then they are worthy of at least serious attention by the historian. In literature there are many different kinds of miracle-stories; but the Gospels do not ask us to believe that Jesus made the sun travel from west to east one day, or anything like that; they do not even attribute to Him such monstrosities as we find in the apocryphal Gospels of the second century. In general, they are 'in character'—that is to say, they are the kind of works that might be expected from such a Person as the Gospels represent Jesus to be. As we have seen, not even in the earliest Gospel strata can we find a non-supernatural Jesus, and we need not be surprised if supernatural works are attributed to Him. If we reject from the start the idea of a supernatural Jesus, then we shall reject His miracles, too; if, on the other hand, we accept the Gospel picture of Him, the miracles will cease to be an insuperable stumbling-block.

No doubt, the historian will be more exacting in his examination of the evidence where miracles are in question. But if the evidence is really good, he will not refuse it on *a priori* grounds. Thus, in a book which treats the life of Jesus from the purely historical viewpoint, Professor A. T. Olmstead, a leading authority on ancient Oriental history, says with regard to the account

THE GOSPEL MIRACLES

63

of the raising of Lazarus in John xi, which he accepts
as the narrative of an eyewitness: 'As with so many
accounts found in our best sources, the historian can
only repeat it, without seeking for psychological or other
explanations.'[1] This may not satisfy the physicist or the
psychologist; for the matter of that, it does not satisfy
the theologian. But it shows that the historical method
has its limitations, just as the scientific method in general
has, when it is confronted with a phenomenon which is
by its very nature unique.

Again, the miracle-stories of the Gospels can be
studied in terms of Form Criticism; they can be compared with stories of similar wonders in literature or
folklore, and various interesting inferences can be drawn
from a comparative examination of this kind. But this
approach will not lead us to firm conclusions about the
historical character of the Gospel miracles, nor will it
explain the significance which these miracles have in the
context of the life and activity of Jesus.

Our first concern about the Gospel miracles should be
not to 'defend' them but to understand them. And when
we have learned to do that, we shall find that their
defence can take care of itself. The centre of the gospel
is Christ Himself; we must view the miracles in the
light of His person. It is thus really beside the point to
demonstrate how as a matter of fact many of those
miracles are in the light of modern science not so
'impossible' after all. Interesting as it may be to re-state
the healing narratives in terms of faith-healing or
psycho-therapy, this will not help us to appreciate their
significance in the Gospel record. One very popular
preacher and writer has dealt with several of the
miracles from the psychological point of view in a very
able way, without always carrying conviction, as when,
for example, he traces the trouble of the man possessed
with a *legion* of demons[2] back to a dreadful day in his

[1] *Jesus in the Light of History*, p. 206. See p. 49.

[2] See the discussion of demon-possession by Professor A. R. Short,
M.D., B.Sc., F.R.C.S., in *Modern Discovery and the Bible* (I.V.F., 1943),
pp. 89 ff.; *The Bible and Modern Medicine* (1953), pp. 109 ff.

A minor point in connection with the Legion story, though not so
important as the healing of the demoniac or the destruction of the

childhood when he saw a *legion* of soldiers massacring the infants of Bethlehem, or another dreadful scene of the same kind. If this sort of argument helps some people to believe the Gospel record who otherwise would not believe it, so far so good. They may even be willing to accept the stories of raising the dead, in view of well-authenticated cases of people who have been technically dead for a few minutes and have then been restored to life.

These may make it easier for some people to believe in the raising of Jairus' daughter, or even of the young man of Nain, but they will hardly fit the case of Lazarus, who had been four days in the grave. And these other raisings of the dead remind us of the chief Gospel miracle of all, the resurrection of Jesus Himself. Attempts have been made to rationalize or explain away the resurrection story from the very beginning, when the detachment of the temple guard deputed to watch His tomb were bribed by the chief priests to say : 'His disciples came by night, and stole him away while we slept' (Mt. xxviii. 13). That was but the first of many rationalizations. Others have suggested that Jesus did not really die. George Moore treated this theme imaginatively in *The Brook Kerith,* but when we read it we realize that such a situation could have had nothing to do with the historical rise of Christianity. Other suggestions are that it was the wrong grave that the women

pigs, is of interest as illustrating the danger of criticizing statements in the Gospels on a basis of inadequate information. It concerns the name of the place where the incident took place. According to the best texts, Matthew calls it 'the country of the Gadarenes' (viii. 28); Mark, 'the country of the Gerasenes' (v. 1), and Luke, probably, 'the country of the Gergesenes' (viii. 26). T. H. Huxley, in his *Essays upon some Controverted Questions* (1892), made merry over the escapade of the Gadarene swine, running the seven miles between Gadara and the Lake of Galilee, crossing the deep river Yarmuk *en route.* The best known Gerasa was a Greek city nearly forty miles south-east of the lake (modern Jerash in Transjordan); but the name of Mark's Gerasa survives in the modern village of Kersa, on the east shore of the lake. Luke's reading 'Gergesenes' may represent even more accurately the ancient name of this place, as Origen knew of a Gergesa on the Lake of Galilee. But the city of Gadara owned some territory round about Kersa, so that the district and the pigs could properly also be called Gadarene.

went to; or that the Jewish authorities themselves had the body removed, lest it or the grave should become a centre of devotion and a cause of further trouble. Or the disciples all with one consent became the victims of hallucination, or experienced something quite extraordinary in the nature of extra-sensory perception. (The idea that they deliberately invented the tale is very properly discountenanced as a moral and psychological impossibility.) But the one interpretation which best accounts for all the data, as well as for the abiding sequel, is that Jesus' bodily resurrection from the dead was a real and objective event.[1]

As regards details of time and place, some well-known difficulties arise when we compare the various accounts of resurrection appearances. Some of these difficulties might be more easily solved if we knew how the Gospel of Mark originally ended. As appears from the textual evidence, the original ending of this Gospel may have been lost at a very early date, and the narrative breaks off short at xvi. 8. (The verses which follow in our Bibles are a later appendix.) But when we have taken note of the difficulty of harmonizing all the accounts, we are confronted with a hard core of historical fact: (*a*) the tomb was really empty; (*b*) the Lord appeared to various individuals and groups of disciples both in Judæa and in Galilee; (*c*) the Jewish authorities could not disprove the disciples' claim that He had risen from the dead.

When, some fifty days after the crucifixion, the disciples began their public proclamation of the gospel, they put forward as the chief argument for their claims about Jesus the fact of His rising from the dead. 'We saw Him alive,' they asserted. Paul quotes the summary of the evidence which he himself received: 'He appeared to Cephas [*i.e.* Peter], then to the Twelve; then He appeared to above five hundred brethren at once, of whom the greater part remain until now [*c.* AD 55, about twenty-five years after the crucifixion], but some are fallen asleep; then He appeared to James [His brother],

[1] I have treated these questions in greater detail in *The Spreading Flame*, pp. 59 ff.

then to all the apostles' (see 1 Cor. xv. 5-7). It is note-worthy that in their *public* references to the resurrection they did not appeal to the testimony of the women who had actually been first at the sepulchre; it would have been too easy to answer : 'Oh, we know what value to attach to the visions of excitable women!'

As it was, the public proclamation of Christ as risen, and as therefore demonstrably the Messiah and Son of God, made an immediate and deep impression on the Jerusalem populace, so much so that the priestly authori-ties had soon to take steps in an attempt to check the new movement. But they were unsuccessful. If, however, Jesus had really not risen, they could surely have pro-vided sufficient evidence to prove it. They had all the necessary power, and it was to the interest of the Roman authorities to help them. It could not have been such an insuperable difficulty to find and produce the body of Jesus, dead or (only just) alive. It was to the interest of the Sanhedrin to produce His body, or else to procure certified evidence of its disposal. The fact that the first story put about to counter the Christians' claim was that the disciples had stolen the body simply means that the Sanhedrin did not know what had happened to it. It must be remembered that to the apostles and their opponents alike resurrection meant one thing—resurrec-tion of the body. And if we ask why the Sanhedrin did not sponsor a more convincing story than that of the disciples' theft, the answer no doubt is that (as Arnold Lunn puts it) they knew what they could get away with.[1] They must have reviewed and regretfully dis-missed several beautiful hypotheses before they settled on this as the least improbable one.

But, while Christ's resurrection was proclaimed by the early Christians as a historical event, it had more than a merely historical significance for them. First of all, it was the grand demonstration of the Messiahship of Jesus. It did not *make* Him Messiah, but it proved that He was Messiah. As Paul says, He was 'declared to be the Son of God with power, . . . by the resurrec-tion of the dead' (Rom. i. 4). Again, it was the grand

[1] A. Lunn, *The Third Day* (1945), p. 89.

demonstration of the power of God. That power had been displayed many times in the world's history, but never with such magnificent completeness as in the resurrection of Christ. Nor is this display of God's power simply an event in history; it has a personal meaning for every Christian, for the same victorious power that raised Jesus from the dead is the power which operates in His followers, achieving in their lives triumph over the dominion of evil. Properly to appreciate the power of God in the resurrection of Christ, one must appreciate it in one's own experience. That is why Paul prayed that he might thus know Christ, and 'the power of his resurrection' (Phil. iii. 10).

Jesus on the cross had been a spectacle of foolishness and weakness, so far as the eyes of men could see. But when we look at the cross in the light of the resurrection, then we see in Christ crucified the power and the wisdom of God. And only thus can we properly consider the miracle-stories of the Gospels. If Christ is the power of God, then these stories, far from being an obstacle to belief, appear natural and reasonable; from Him who was the power of God incarnate, we naturally expect manifestations of divine power. Our estimate of the miracles will depend on our estimate of Christ. They are related in the Gospel record just because they are illustrations of that power which was supremely revealed in the resurrection and which in the gospel is freely put at the disposal of all believers. Seen from this point of view, the miracle-stories appear instinct with evangelical significance.

So the question whether the miracle-stories of the Gospels are true cannot be answered purely in terms of historical research. Historical research is by no means excluded, for the whole point of the gospel is that in Christ the power and grace of God entered into human history to bring about the world's redemption. But a historian may conclude that these things probably did happen and yet be quite far from the response which the recorders of these events wished to evoke in those whom they addressed. The question whether the miracle-stories are true must ultimately be answered by a personal response of faith—not merely faith in the events as historical but faith in the Christ who performed them, faith which appropriates the power by which these mighty works were done.

This response of faith does not absolve us from the duty of understanding the special significance of the several miracle-stories and considering each in the light of all the available knowledge, historical and otherwise, which can be brought to bear upon it. But these are secondary duties; the primary one is to see the whole question in its proper context as revealed by the significance of the greatest miracle of all, the resurrection of Christ.

If we do proceed to ask what the independent non-Christian evidence for the Gospel miracles is, we shall find that early non-Christian writers who do refer to Jesus at any length do not dispute that He performed miracles. Josephus, as we shall see, calls Him a wonder-worker; later Jewish references in the rabbinical writings, as we shall also see, attribute His miracles to sorcery, but do not deny them, just as some in the days of His flesh attributed His powers to demon-possession. Sorcery is also the explanation given by Celsus, the philosophic critic of Christianity in the second century.[1] The early apostles referred to His miracles as facts which their audiences were as well acquainted with as they themselves were; similarly the early apologists refer to them as events beyond dispute by the opponents of Christianity.[2]

The healing miracles we have already touched upon; they generally present little difficulty nowadays, but the so-called 'nature miracles' are in a different category. Here in particular our approach to the question will be dictated by our attitude to Christ Himself. If He was in truth the power of God, then we need not be surprised to find real creative acts performed by Him. If He was not, then we must fall back on some such explanation as misunderstanding or hallucination on the part of the

---

[1] Origen, *Contra Celsum* i. 38; ii. 48.

[2] *E.g.* Quadratus, in his *Apologia* addressed to the Emperor Hadrian in AD 133 (Eusebius, *H.E.* iv. 3).

witnesses, or imposture, or corruption of the records in the course of their transmission or the like.

Take the story of the changing of the water into wine in John ii, a story in many ways unique among the miracle-stories of the Gospels. It is possible to treat it as one writer does, who suggests that the water remained water all the time, but that Jesus had it served up as wine in a spirit of good-humoured playfulness, while the master of the ceremonies, entering into the spirit of the harmless practical joke, says : 'Of course, the best wine! Adam's wine! But why have you kept the best till now?' —but to do so betrays an almost incredible capacity for missing the whole point and context of the story, while it is ludicrous to link such an account with the following words : 'This beginning of signs did Jesus in Cana of Galilee, and manifested his glory' (verse 11), to say nothing of its irrelevance for the purpose of the fourth Gospel : 'These things are written that you may believe that Jesus is the Messiah, the Son of God' (Jn. xx. 31). Such a reconstruction is not even worthy to be dignified with the name of rationalization. Whatever difficulties the story as it is told by John may contain, it is clear that something of a very wonderful and impressive nature happened, in which the disciples saw the glory of God revealed in their Master.

'This beginning of signs did Jesus.' The miracles of the fourth Gospel are always called 'signs', and elsewhere in the New Testament the word for 'miracle' or 'wonder' is regularly linked with the word for 'sign'. 'Signs and wonders' is a frequent phrase, as if to teach us that the miracles are not related merely for their capacity of begetting wonder in the hearers and readers, but also because of what they signified. Our Lord did not esteem very highly the kind of belief that arose simply from witnessing miracles.[1] His desire was that men should realize what these things signified. They were signs of the messianic age, such as had been foretold by the prophets of old. So also are the miracles in Acts, for they, too, are wrought in the name of Jesus and by His power, transmitted through His apostles. They are

[1] *Cf.* Jn. ii. 23-25, vi. 26.

'mighty works', signifying that the power of God has entered into human life; they are 'the powers of the age to come' (Heb. vi. 5), signifying that the age to come has in Christ invaded this present age. Many people were simply attracted by the wonder of these deeds, but others saw what they signified, and could say with John : 'The Word became flesh, and pitched his tabernacle among us; and *we beheld his glory*' (see Jn. i. 14).

Thus the healing miracles were signs of the messianic age, for was it not written in Isaiah xxxv. 5 f. : 'Then the eyes of the blind shall be opened, and the ears of the deaf shall be unstopped. Then shall the lame man leap like a hart, and the tongue of the dumb shall sing'? Besides, the power that was effective in conquering these ailments was the same power that could prevail over evil in all its forms; the authority by which Christ said to the paralytic, 'Rise, take up your bed, and walk,' was the same authority by which He said, 'Son, your sins are forgiven.' The visible operation of His healing power was the evident token of His forgiving power (Mk. ii. 10 f.). So, then, all the miracles of healing are in a sense parables of the soul's deliverance from sin, and therefore the prominent place they occupy in the Gospel story is amply justified.

So also the nature miracles were signs of the messianic age, which was to be a time of unprecedented fruitfulness; this was betokened by the sign of the wine and the multiplication of the bread. The messianic age was also depicted as a marriage-feast, and the miracle performed by Jesus at the marriage in Cana was thus a sign of the abundant joy of that age, a token that, as He and His disciples proclaimed, the kingdom of heaven had drawn near. It also signified that in spite of the proverb, 'The old is better,' the new order which He came to introduce was as superior to the old order of Judaism as wine is superior to water.

The other great nature miracle is the feeding of the multitude with the loaves and fishes. There are two narratives of this kind in the first two Gospels, one where 5,000 were fed with five loaves and two fishes (Mt. xiv. 15 ff.; Mk. vi. 35 ff.), and another where 4,000 were fed with seven loaves and a few fishes (Mt. xv. 32 ff.; Mk. viii. 1 ff.). These have frequently been taken for duplicate accounts of one event, but this is an over-simplification. These two feedings belong respectively to two parallel series of similar incidents, one series being enacted on Jewish soil, the other on Gentile soil to the north and east of Galilee. The incidents are selected in order to show how Jesus repeated on this occasion among the Gentiles acts which He performed among the Jews. Indeed, it has been suggested that there is significance in the difference between the two words for 'basket' used in the two accounts, the one in the first account being a basket with special Jewish associations, that in the second account being a more general word. Since Peter was the chief authority behind the second Gospel, it is not incredible that the apostle who used the keys of the kingdom of heaven to open the door of faith, to the Jew first and then to the Gentile, should have related these two similar miracles in his gospel preaching to show how Christ was the bread of life for Gentiles as for Jews.

The feeding miracles, according to the plain sense of the narrative, were acts of superhuman power. In truth, to rationalize them robs them of all point. It is easy to say that the example of the boy's handing over his bread and fish led all the others to share their provisions too, so that there was enough for all; but that is not the Gospel story. Here, again, our estimate of Christ makes all the difference to our approach to the miracle. The multiplication of the loaves was a token of the messianic feast; it signified the abundance of provision that men might find in Christ, the true bread of God. If the bread represents the harvest of the land, the fish will represent the harvest of the sea. We may recall, moreover, the early Church's use of the fish as a symbol of Christ. In any case, the majority of those who saw the miracle saw it as a miracle only; but it is rather striking that in Mark Jesus helps His disciples to understand the real significance of the multiplication of the bread in a passage (Mk. viii. 19-21) which comes only a few verses before the declaration of Peter at Cæsarea Philippi :

'When I broke the five loaves among the 5,000, how many
baskets full of fragments did you take up? They say to him,
Twelve. And when I broke the seven among the 4,000, how
many baskets full of fragments did you take up? They answer,
Seven. And he said to them, Do you not understand
yet?'

Between these words and the incident at Cæsarea
Philippi comes, significantly enough, the healing of the
blind man of Bethsaida who received his sight gradually,
first seeing men as trees walking, and then seeing all
things clearly (Mk. viii. 22 ff.)—a parable of the disciples, who had hitherto perceived His Messiahship
dimly, but were now, through their spokesman Peter, to
declare outright, 'You are the Messiah.' Was it not this
that Jesus meant when He asked, 'Do you not understand *yet?*' And was not this the great truth of which
the feeding miracles, like all the others, were signs?

Two more miracles may be mentioned, as both have
been widely misunderstood. The one is the story of the
coin in the fish's mouth (Mt. xvii. 24 ff.). This has been
dealt with in terms of Form Criticism. The question
must frequently have arisen in the early Jerusalem
church, whether the Jewish Christians should continue
to pay the temple tax, the half-shekel due from each
adult Jewish male. According to some Form critics, they
came to the conclusion that, although they were under
no obligation to pay it, they would do so, lest they
should cause offence to their fellow-Jews. This, then,
was the 'life-setting' of the story. But when we are told
that, by a sort of legal fiction, the decision was thrown
back into the lifetime of Jesus so as to be invested with
His authority, we must demur. The whole question came
to an end with the destruction of the temple in AD 70,
and when it was debated in the Jerusalem church there
must have been many who would have a good idea
whether such a thing had taken place in Jesus' lifetime
or not. The 'life-setting' in the Jerusalem church is
probable enough; but what it explains is not the inven-
tion of the story, but its recording. When the problem
of the temple tax arose, the natural question was : 'Did
our Master say anything about this? Did He pay the

half-shekel?' Then the incident was remembered, and recorded for a precedent. A 'life-setting' in the early Church does not preclude a prior 'life-setting' in the life of Jesus Himself.

But, apart from what the story signifies, some have felt a difficulty in the miracle implied in the words of Jesus with which the incident closes. (We are not told that Peter did find a coin in the fish's mouth; but we are clearly intended to understand that he did.) It is, again, easy to say that Peter caught a fish which he sold for a shekel, thus getting enough to pay his own tax and his Master's, and this time the rationalization does not greatly impair the significance of the story. But some rationalizers seem to suppose that the miracle consisted in Peter's finding the coin in the fish's mouth. There was nothing miraculous in that; such objects have often been found in the mouths or stomachs of fish.[1] The 'miracle', if such it be, is that Jesus knew in advance that Peter would find the coin there,[2] so that once more we are brought to realize that we must first make up our minds about Christ before coming to conclusions about the miracles attributed to Him.

The other miracle is the cursing of the barren fig tree (Mk. xi. 12 ff.), a stumbling-block to many. They feel that it is unlike Jesus, and so someone must have misunderstood what actually happened, or turned a spoken parable into an acted miracle, or something like that. Some, on the other hand, welcome the story because it shows that Jesus was human enough to get unreasonably annoyed on occasion. It appears, however, that a closer acquaintance with fig trees would have prevented such misunderstandings. 'The time of figs was not yet,' says

---

[1] There is a well-known fish called the *musht* in the Sea of Galilee addicted to this sort of thing. 'These fish . . . have habits like your English magpie. They are attracted by anything sparkling or bright. The natives often find bits of glass, or metal, or stone, or a coin, in their mouths' (L. D. Weatherhead, *It Happened in Palestine* [1936], p. 36). For this reason the fish is sometimes called St. Peter's fish.

[2] Possibly we are also intended to understand that He knew of the collectors' question and Peter's answer without overhearing or being told.

Mark, for it was just before Passover, about six weeks before the fully-formed fig appears. The fact that Mark adds these words shows that he knew what he was talking about. When the fig-leaves appear about the end of March they are accompanied by a crop of small knobs, called *taqsh* by the Arabs, a sort of fore-runner of the real figs. These *taqsh* are eaten by peasants and others when hungry. They drop off before the real fig is formed. But if the leaves appear unaccompanied by *taqsh*, there will be no figs that year. So it was evident to our Lord, when He turned aside to see if there were any of these *taqsh* on the fig-tree to assuage His hunger for the time being, that the absence of the *taqsh* meant that there would be no figs when the time for figs came. For all its fair show of foliage, it was a fruitless and hopeless tree.[1]

The whole incident was an acted parable. To Jesus the fig-tree, fair but barren, spoke of the city of Jerusalem, where He had found much religious observance, but no response to His message from God. The withering of the tree was thus an omen of the disaster which, as He foresaw and foretold, would shortly fall upon the city.

But, as Mark records the incident, the withering of the tree had a personal significance for the disciples; it taught them to have faith in God (Mk. xi. 22). And this is the moral which the miracle-stories have for us today. They are recorded as signs of divine power; and even if we could prove their historicity up to the hilt we should still miss the point of their narration if we failed to see in them tokens of the activity of God in history, culminating in the appearance of Christ on earth. As the Gospel parables are oral lessons of the kingdom of God, so the Gospel miracles are object lessons, acted parables of the kingdom. Like the Gospel story as a whole, they challenge us to have faith in God, as He is revealed in Christ. When we turn from our attempts at rationalizing them so as to make them more acceptable to the spirit of our age, and try rather to understand why they were recorded by the evangelists, we shall be in a position to

[1] *Cf.* W. M. Christie, *Palestine Calling* (1939), pp. 118 ff.

profit by them as the evangelists intended we should. We shall learn then by experience 'that it is true of the miracle-stories, as of every part of the gospel record, that "these things were written that ye might believe that Jesus is the Christ, the Son of God, and that believing ye might have life in His name" (Jn. xx. 31)'.[1]

[1] These are the concluding words of Professor Alan Richardson's *The Miracle-Stories of the Gospels* (1941), a book to which I am greatly indebted for light on the subject-matter of this chapter. Another book on the same subject which has been very helpful to many students is D. S. Cairns, *The Faith that Rebels* (1929).

CHAPTER 6

THE IMPORTANCE
OF PAUL'S EVIDENCE

THE earliest of the New Testament writings, as they
have come down to us, are the letters written by
the apostle Paul up to the time of his detention in
Rome (*c.* AD 60-62). The earliest of our Gospels in its
present form can certainly not be dated earlier than AD
60, but from the hand of Paul we have ten Epistles written
between 48 and 60.

This man Paul was a Roman citizen of Jewish birth
(his Jewish name was Saul), born somewhere about the
commencement of the Christian era in the city of Tarsus
in Cilicia, Asia Minor. His birthplace, 'no mean city',
as he said himself (Acts xxi. 39), was in those days an
eminent centre of Greek culture, which did not fail to
leave its mark on Paul, as may be seen in his speeches
and letters. He received an education in Jerusalem under
Gamaliel,[1] the greatest Rabbi of his day and a leader of
the party of the Pharisees. He rapidly attained distinction among his contemporaries by the diligence of his
studies and the fervour with which he upheld the
ancestral traditions of the Jewish nation.[2] He may even
—though this is uncertain—have been a member of the
Sanhedrin, the supreme court of the nation.

This zeal for the law brought him into conflict with
the early Jerusalem Christians, especially with those
who belonged to the circle of Stephen, whose teaching
he must have heard in the synagogue where the Cilician
Jews met[3] and who early realized, with exceptionally
far-sighted comprehension, that the gospel cut at the
roots of the traditional Jewish ceremonial law and cultus.
At the stoning of Stephen, we find Paul playing a
responsible part and giving his consent to his death, and
thereafter proceeding to uproot the new movement

[1] Acts xxii. 3. [2] Gal. i. 13 f. [3] Acts vi. 9.

which, in his eyes, stood revealed by Stephen's activity as a deadly threat to all that he counted dear in Judaism.[1] To use his own words, 'Beyond all measure I persecuted the Church of God and harried it' (see Gal. i. 13)—until his encounter with Jesus on the road to Damascus convinced his mind and conscience of the reality of His resurrection, and therewith of the validity of the Christians' claims, whereupon he became the chief herald of the faith of which he formerly made havoc.

It is reasonable to believe that the evidence which convinced such a man of the out-and-out wrongness of his former course, and led him so decisively to abandon previously cherished beliefs for a movement which he had so vigorously opposed, must have been of a singularly impressive quality. The conversion of Paul has for long been regarded as a weighty evidence for the truth of Christianity. Many have endorsed the conclusion of the eighteenth-century statesman George, Lord Lyttelton, that 'the conversion and apostleship of St. Paul alone, duly considered, was of itself a demonstration sufficient to prove Christianity to be a divine revelation'.[2]

Here, however, we are chiefly concerned with the information we can derive from his Epistles. These were not written to record the facts of the life and ministry of Jesus; they were addressed to Christians, who already knew the gospel story. Yet in them we can find sufficient material to construct an outline of the early apostolic preaching about Jesus. While Paul insists on the divine pre-existence of Jesus,[3] yet he knows that He was none the less a real human being,[4] a descendant of Abra-

---

[1] Acts vii. 58, viii. 1 ff., ix. 1 ff., xxii. 4, xxvi. 9 ff.; 1 Cor. xv. 9, etc.

[2] In his *Observations on the Conversion of St. Paul*, of which work Dr. Samuel Johnson wrote: 'He had, in the pride of juvenile confidence, with the help of corrupt conversation, entertained doubts of the truth of Christianity; but he thought the time now come when it was no longer fit to doubt or believe by chance, and applied himself seriously to the great question. His studies being honest, ended in conviction. He found that religion was true; and what he had learned he endeavoured to teach (1747) by *Observations on the Conversion of St. Paul*; a treatise to which infidelity has never been able to fabricate a specious answer' (*Lives of the Poets: Lyttelton*).

[3] *E.g.* Col. i. 15 ff.

[4] Gal. iv. 4.

ham[1] and David[2]; who lived under the Jewish law[3]; who was betrayed, and on the night of His betrayal instituted a memorial meal of bread and wine[4]; who endured the Roman penalty of crucifixion,[5] although the responsibility for His death is laid at the door of the representatives of the Jewish nation[6]; who was buried, rose the third day, and was thereafter seen alive by many eyewitnesses on various occasions, including one occasion on which He was so seen by over five hundred at once, of whom the majority were alive nearly twenty-five years later.[7] In this summary of the evidence for the reality of Christ's resurrection, Paul shows a sound instinct for the necessity of marshalling personal testimony in support of what might well appear an incredible assertion.

Paul knows of the Lord's apostles,[8] of whom Peter and John are mentioned by name as 'pillars' of the Jerusalem community,[9] and of His brothers, of whom James is similarly mentioned.[10] He knows that the Lord's brothers and apostles, including Peter, were married[11] —an incidental agreement with the Gospel story of the healing of Peter's mother-in-law.[12] He quotes sayings of Jesus on occasion—*e.g.*, His teaching on marriage and divorce,[13] and on the right of gospel preachers to have their material needs supplied[14]; and the words He used at the institution of the Lord's Supper.[15]

Even where he does not quote the actual sayings of Jesus, he shows throughout his works how well acquainted he was with them. In particular, we ought to compare the ethical section of the Epistle to the Romans (xii. 1 to xv. 7), where Paul summarizes the practical implications of the gospel for the lives of believers, with the Sermon on the Mount, to see how thoroughly imbued the apostle was with the teaching of his Master. Besides, there and elsewhere Paul's chief argument in his ethical instruction is the example of

[1] Rom. ix. 5. [2] Rom. i. 3. [3] Gal. iv. 4.
[4] 1 Cor. xi. 23 ff. [5] Phil. ii. 8; 1 Cor. i. 23; Gal. iii. 13, vi. 14, etc.
[6] 1 Thes. ii. 15. [7] 1 Cor. xv. 4 ff. [8] Gal. i. 17 ff.
[9] Gal. ii. 9. [10] Gal. i. 19, ii. 9. [11] 1 Cor. ix. 5.
[12] Mk. i. 30. [13] 1 Cor. vii. 10 f.
[14] 1 Cor. ix. 14; 1 Tim. v. 18; *cf.* Lk. x. 7.

Christ Himself. And the character of Christ as understood by Paul is in perfect agreement with His character
as portrayed in the Gospels. When Paul speaks of 'the
meekness and gentleness of Christ' (2 Cor. x. 1), we
remember our Lord's own words, 'I am meek and lowly
in heart' (Mt. xi. 29). The self-denying Christ of the
Gospels is the one of whom Paul says, 'Even Christ
pleased not himself' (Rom. xv. 3); and just as the Christ
of the Gospels called on His followers to deny themselves (Mk. viii. 34), so the apostle insists that, after the
example of Christ Himself, it is our Christian duty 'to
bear the infirmities of the weak, and not to please ourselves' (Rom. xv. 1). He who said : 'I am among you
as the servant' (Lk. xxii. 27), and performed the menial
task of washing His disciples' feet (Jn. xiii. 4 ff.), is He
who, according to Paul, 'took the form of a slave' (Phil.
ii. 7). In a word, when Paul wishes to commend to his
readers all those moral graces which adorn the Christ
of the Gospels he does so in language like this : 'Put on
the Lord Jesus Christ' (Rom. xiii. 14).

In short, the outline of the gospel story as we can
trace it in the writings of Paul agrees with the outline
which we find elsewhere in the New Testament, and in
the four Gospels in particular. Paul himself is at pains to
point out that the gospel which he preached was one
and the same gospel as that preached by the other
apostles[1]—a striking claim, considering that Paul was
neither a companion of Christ in the days of His flesh
nor of the original apostles, and that he vigorously
asserts his complete independence of these.[2]

[1] 1 Cor. xv. 11.

[2] For the subject of this chapter see also C. H. Dodd, *History and
the Gospel* (1938), pp. 63 ff.; and A. M. Hunter, *Paul and his Predecessors* (1961); but above all, J. G. Machen, *The Origin of Paul's
Religion* (1921, reprinted 1947), and S. Kim, *The Origin of Paul's
Gospel* (1981). I have dealt with it more fully in *Paul and Jesus*
(1974) and *Paul: Apostle of the Free Spirit* (1977), pp. 95-112.

CHAPTER 7

THE WRITINGS OF LUKE

OUTSIDE Paul's own letters, we have most of our information about him from the writings of his friend and companion Luke, the author of the third Gospel and the Acts of the Apostles. Luke was a physician by profession,[1] and according to a tradition which can be traced back to the second century was a native of Antioch in Syria.[2] Some support is given to this tradition by the internal evidence of his writings. So far as we can tell, he was the only Gentile among the New Testament writers. His two works are really two parts of one continuous historical work, carrying the history of Christian origins from the time of John the Baptist down to about the year 60.

Both parts of this work are addressed to an otherwise unknown person named Theophilus, who apparently had some previous knowledge of Christianity, and may have been a person of some official status, seeing that Luke gives him the title 'most excellent'—the same title as that by which Paul addresses Felix and Festus, the Roman governors of Judæa. In the prologue to his Gospel Luke explains the purpose of his twofold work in these words :

'Most excellent Theophilus! Since many have undertaken to draw up a narrative of the things that have been accomplished among us, as they have been transmitted to us by those who from the beginning were eyewitnesses and ministers of the Word, I too, having followed the whole course of events accurately from the first, have decided to write an orderly account for you, in order that you may be sure of the reliability of the information which you have received' (Lk. I. 1-4).

Luke inherited the high traditions of Greek historical writing, and had access to various excellent sources of

[1] Col. iv. 14.
[2] Anti-Marcionite prologue to Luke; also Eusebius, *H.E.* iii. 4.

information about the events with which he dealt, besides being himself present at some of the incidents which he narrated. We have already mentioned some of the sources, written and oral, on which he may have drawn.[1] The value of his work may be realized if we compare our relatively[2] ample knowledge of the progress of Christianity before AD 60 with our ignorance of it for many years after that date; indeed, after Luke there arose no writer who can really be called a historian of the Christian Church until Eusebius, whose *Ecclesiastical History* was written after Constantine's Milan Edict of Toleration (AD 313).

Whatever his sources were, Luke made good use of them. And he sets his story in the context of imperial history. Of all the New Testament writers, he is the only one who so much as names a Roman emperor. Three emperors (Augustus, Tiberius, and Claudius)[3] are mentioned by name; the Emperor Nero is also referred to, but not by his personal name—he is the 'Cæsar' to whom Paul appealed.[4] The birth of Jesus is fixed in the reign of the Emperor Augustus, when Herod the Great was king of Judæa, at the time of an imperial census.[5] The commencement of the public ministry of John the Baptist, with which the apostolic preaching begins, is elaborately dated by a series of synchronisms in the Greek historical manner,[6] reminding the classical student of the synchronisms with which, for example, Thucydides dates the formal outbreak of the Peloponnesian War in the beginning of the second book of his *History*. Names of note in the Jewish and Gentile world of his day appear in Luke's pages; in addition to the emperors, we meet the Roman governors Quirinius, Pilate, Sergius Paullus, Gallio, Felix, and Festus; Herod the Great and some of his descendants—Herod Antipas the tetrarch of

[1] See pp. 41 ff.
[2] But only 'relatively', because Luke traces the progress of the gospel mainly along the route from Jerusalem to Rome; we have little or no information about the simultaneous missionary activity in Africa or in non-Roman Asia.
[3] Lk. ii. 1, iii. 1; Acts xi. 28 and xviii. 2.
[4] Acts xxv. 11, etc.; he is called Augustus in xxv. 21.
[5] Lk. i. 5, ii. 1 f. See p. 87.   [6] Lk. iii. 1 f.

Galilee, the vassal-kings Herod Agrippa I and II, Berenice and Drusilla; leading members of the Jewish priestly caste such as Annas, Caiaphas, and Ananias; Gamaliel, the greatest contemporary Rabbi and Pharisaic leader. A writer who thus relates his story to the wider context of world history is courting trouble if he is not careful; he affords his critical readers so many opportunities for testing his accuracy.

Luke takes this risk, and stands the test admirably. One of the most remarkable tokens of his accuracy is his sure familiarity with the proper titles of all the notable persons who are mentioned in his pages. This was by no means such an easy feat in his days as it is in ours, when it is so simple to consult convenient books of reference. The accuracy of Luke's use of the various titles in the Roman Empire has been compared to the easy and confident way in which an Oxford man in ordinary conversation will refer to the Heads of Oxford colleges by their proper titles—the *Provost* of Oriel, the *Master* of Balliol, the *Rector* of Exeter, the *President* of Magdalen, and so on. A non-Oxonian like the present writer never feels quite at home with the multiplicity of these Oxford titles. But Luke had a further difficulty in that the titles sometimes did not remain the same for any great length of time; a province might pass from senatorial government to administration by a direct representative of the emperor, and would then be governed no longer by a proconsul but by an imperial legate (*legatus pro prætore*).

Cyprus, for example, which was an imperial province until 22 BC, became a senatorial province in that year, and was therefore governed no longer by an imperial legate but by a proconsul. And so, when Paul and Barnabas arrived in Cyprus about AD 47, it was the *proconsul* Sergius Paullus whom they met (Acts xiii. 7), a man of whom we know a little more through inscriptions, and in whose family Sir William Ramsay claimed that Christianity could be traced at a later date.[1]

---

[1] *The Bearing of Recent Discovery on the Trustworthiness of the New Testament* (1915), pp. 150 ff.; cf. F. F. Bruce, *Paul: Apostle of the Free Spirit* (1977), p. 161.

Similarly the governors of Achaia and Asia are pro-consuls, as both these provinces were senatorial. Gallio, the proconsul of Achaia (Acts xviii. 12), is known to us as the brother of Seneca, the great Stoic philosopher and tutor of Nero. An inscription at Delphi, in central Greece, recording a proclamation of the Emperor Claudius, indicates that Gallio became proconsul of Achaia in July, AD 51. Achaia was a senatorial province from 27 BC to AD 15, and again from AD 44 onwards. It is noteworthy that Luke, who generally calls countries by their ethnic or popular names rather than by Roman provincial nomenclature, and who elsewhere calls the province of Achaia by its more ordinary name Greece (Acts xx. 2), departs from his custom when giving a governor's official title, and so calls Gallio not 'proconsul of Greece' but 'proconsul of Achaia'—his official title.

The reference to the proconsuls of Asia in Acts xix. 38 is strange. There was only one proconsul at a time, and yet the town-clerk of Ephesus says to the riotous con-course of citizens, 'There are proconsuls.' We might say that this is the 'generalizing plural', but would it not have been simpler to say, 'There is the proconsul'? An examination of the chronological data, however, reveals that only a few months before the riot in the Ephesian theatre the proconsul of Asia, Junius Silanus, had been assassinated by emissaries of Agrippina, the mother of Nero, who had just become emperor (AD 54).[1] A suc-cessor to Silanus had not yet arrived, and this by itself would account for the town-clerk's indefinite reference, 'There are proconsuls'; but it is also tempting to take the words as referring to Helius and Celer, the murderers of Silanus, for they were in charge of the emperor's affairs in Asia and may well have discharged the pro-consular duties during the interval between the death of Silanus and the arrival of his successor.[2]

The town-clerk of Ephesus was a native official, who acted as the link between the municipal government of the city and the Roman administration. The Asiarchs, who are mentioned on the same occasion (Acts xix. 31),

[1] Tacitus, *Annals* xiii. 1; Dio Cassius, *Hist.* lxi. 6.
[2] *Cf.* G. S. Duncan, *St. Paul's Ephesian Ministry* (1929), pp. 102 ff.

were representatives of the cities of the province who presided over the provincial cult of 'Rome and the Emperor'. Principal Duncan suggests[1] that the riot took place at the Ephesian festival of Artemisia, held in March or April in honour of the goddess Artemis (the Diana of the English AV); the Asiarchs, as chief priests of the imperial cult, would naturally be present at such a festival to represent the emperor.

The city of Ephesus itself is given the title *Neōkoros*, 'Warden of the Temple' of Artemis (Acts xix. 35). This word literally means 'temple-sweeper', but came to be given as a title of honour, first to individuals, and then to cities as well. (Similarly in our own day, the *George Cross*, instituted as an honour for individuals, has been conferred on the island of Malta.) Luke's ascription of the title to Ephesus is corroborated by a Greek inscription which describes this city as 'Temple-Warden of Artemis'.

The theatre of Ephesus, in which the riotous assembly met, has been excavated, and, to judge by its ruins, it seated something like 25,000 persons. As in many other Greek towns, the theatre was the most convenient place for a meeting of the citizen-body. An interesting discovery in the theatre was an inscription of AD 103-104, in Greek and Latin, telling how a Roman official, C. Vibius Salutaris, presented a silver image of Artemis and other statues to be set on their pedestals at each meeting of the *ecclesia* or citizen-body in the theatre. This reminds us of the interest taken in the cult of the goddess, according to Acts xix. 24, by the guild of silversmiths at Ephesus. The 'silver shrines' which they made for Artemis were small niches containing an image of the goddess with her lions beside her. Some of these miniature temples in terra-cotta have survived.

The magistrates of Philippi, which was a Roman colony, are called 'prætors' in Acts, and they are attended by 'lictors' (the 'serjeants' of the AV), by whose rods Paul and Silas had so many stripes inflicted on them (Acts xvi. 12, 20 ff., 35 ff.). The strict title of these colonial magistrates was 'duumvirs'; but they

[1] *Op. cit.*, p. 140.

affected the more grandiloquent title of 'prætors', like the magistrates of another Roman colony, Capua, of whom Cicero says : 'Although they are called duumvirs in the other colonies, these men wished to be called prætors.'[1]

At Thessalonica the chief magistrates are called 'politarchs' (Acts xvii. 6, 9), a title not found in extant classical literature but occurring in inscriptions as a title of magistrates in Macedonian towns, including Thessalonica.

The ancient court of the Areopagus appears in the narrative of Paul's visit to Athens (Acts xvii. 19, 22). It was the most venerable of all Athenian institutions, and had lost most of its ancient power in the fifth century BC, with the growth of Athenian democracy, but it regained much of its prestige under the Roman Empire. In particular, there is evidence that at this time it exercised a certain control over public lecturers,[2] and it was therefore natural that Paul, arriving in Athens with his new doctrine, should be invited to propound it 'in the midst of the Areopagus' (not, as the AV says, on 'Mars' hill', for though that was the place where the court had met in primitive times, and from which it received its name, it no longer assembled there, but in the Royal Colonnade in the Athenian market-place).

The chief official in Malta is called 'the first man of the island' (Acts xxviii. 7), a title vouched for in both Greek and Latin inscriptions as the proper designation of the Roman governor of Malta.

When Paul arrived in Rome, he was handed over, according to one textual tradition, to an official called the 'stratopedarch' (Acts xxviii. 16), identified by the German historian Mommsen with the *princeps peregrinorum,* the commander of the imperial couriers, of whom the centurion Julius (Acts xxvii. 1) appears to have been one.

Herod Antipas, ruler of Galilee in the time of our Lord, seems to have been given the courtesy title of

[1] *De Lege Agraria,* 34.
[2] See Ramsay, *St. Paul the Traveller* (14th ed., 1920), pp. 245 ff.; *The Bearing of Recent Discovery,* etc., pp. 101 ff.

'king' by his Galilæan subjects (*cf.* Mt. xiv. 9; Mk. vi. 14), but unlike his father Herod the Great and his nephew Herod Agrippa I he was not promoted to royal status by the emperor, and had to be content with the lesser title 'tetrarch'. Luke therefore never calls him king, but always tetrarch (*e.g.* Lk. iii. 1, 19).

The reference in Luke ii. 2 to Quirinius as governor of Syria at the time of the birth of Christ (before the death of Herod the Great in 4 BC) has frequently been thought to be an error, because Quirinius is known to have become imperial legate of Syria in AD 6,[1] and to have supervised in that year the enrolment mentioned in Acts v. 37, which provoked the insurrection led by Judas of Galilee. But it is now widely admitted that an earlier enrolment, as described in Luke ii. 1 ff., (*a*) may have taken place in the reign of Herod the Great, (*b*) may have involved the return of everyone to his family home, (*c*) may have formed part of an Empire-wide census, and (*d*) may have been held during a previous governorship of Quirinius over Syria.

(*a*) Josephus informs us that towards the end of Herod's reign (37-34 BC) the Emperor Augustus treated him more as a subject than as a friend,[2] and that all Judæa took an oath of allegiance to Augustus as well as to Herod.[3] The holding of an imperial census in a client kingdom (as Judæa was during Herod's reign) is not unparalleled; in the reign of Tiberius a census was imposed on the client kingdom of Antiochus in eastern Asia Minor.[4]

(*b*) The obligation on all persons to be enrolled at their domiciles of origin, which made it necessary for Joseph to return to Bethlehem, has been illustrated from an edict of AD 104, in which C. Vibius Maximus, Roman prefect of Egypt, gives notice as follows : 'The enrolment by household being at hand, it is necessary to notify all who for any cause whatsoever are away from their administrative divisions to return home in order

---

[1] Josephus, *Antiquities* xviii. 1. 1.
[2] *Ibid.* xvi. 9. 3.
[3] *Ibid.* xvii. 2. 4.
[4] Tacitus, *Annals* vi. 41.

to comply with the customary ordinance of enrolment, and to remain in their own agricultural land.[1]

(c) There is scattered evidence of the holding of enrolments in various parts of the Empire between 11 and 8 BC, the papyrus evidence in the case of Egypt being practically conclusive.

(d) There is good inscriptional evidence that when Quirinius took up office in Syria in AD 6 this was the second occasion on which he served as imperial legate. The first occasion was when he commanded an expedition against the Homanadensians, a mountain tribe of Asia Minor, some time between 12 and 6 BC. But our evidence does not state expressly in which province he was imperial legate at this earlier date. Sir William Ramsay argued that the province was Syria.[2] We have, however, a continuous record of governors of Syria for those years, which leaves no room for Quirinius; Ramsay suggested that he was appointed as additional and extraordinary legate for military purposes. On the other hand, a good case has been made out for believing that his first term of office as imperial legate was passed in Galatia, not in Syria.[3] The question is not yet finally decided, but it may be best to follow those commentators and grammarians who translate Luke ii. 2 as 'This census was before that which Quirinius, governor of Syria, held'.[4]

Another supposed mistake has been detected by some in Luke iii. 1, where Lysanias is said to have been tetrarch of Abilene (west of Damascus) in the fifteenth year of Tiberius (AD 27-28), whereas the only Lysanias of Abilene otherwise known from ancient history bore the title of king and was executed by order of Mark

---

[1] *Cf.* A. Deissmann, *Light from the Ancient East* (1927), pp. 270 ff.

[2] *The Bearing of Recent Discovery on the Trustworthiness of the New Testament* (1915), pp. 275 ff.

[3] *Cf.* R. Syme, 'Galatia and Pamphylia under Augustus', *Klio* xxvii (1934), pp. 122 ff.

[4] *Cf.* N. Turner, *Grammatical Insights into the New Testament* (1965), pp. 23 f. Some scholars would emend 'Quirinius' to 'Saturninus', following Tertullian (*Adv. Marc.* iv. 19), who says that the census in Judaea at the time of Christ's birth was held by Sentius Saturninus (imperial legate of Syria in 8-6 BC).

Antony in 34 BC. Evidence of a later Lysanias who had the status of tetrarch has, however, been forthcoming from an inscription recording the dedication of a temple 'for the salvation of the Lords Imperial and their whole household, by Nymphæus, a freedman of Lysanias the tetrarch'. The reference to 'the Lords Imperial'—a joint title given only to the Emperor Tiberius and his mother Livia, the widow of Augustus—fixes the date of the inscription between AD 14 (the year of Tiberius' accession) and 29 (the year of Livia's death).[1] On the strength of this and other evidence we may well be satisfied with the verdict of the historian Eduard Meyer, that Luke's reference to Lysanias is 'entirely correct'.[2]

We may mention one out of several instances of the light which ancient coins can throw on the New Testament narrative. The date at which the procurator Felix was replaced by Festus (Acts xxiv. 27) has been much debated by historians. But there is evidence that a new coinage was introduced in Judæa in Nero's fifth year (which ended in October of AD 59), and the most natural occasion for its introduction would be just such a change of procurator. With the above-mentioned inscription from Delphi, fixing the date of Gallio's proconsulship of Achaia (and therewith the chronology of Paul's evangelization of Corinth, recorded in Acts xviii), and this numismatic evidence for dating Festus' arrival as procurator of Judæa in AD 59, we are in a position to date some of the most crucial landmarks in Paul's career. The framework thus provided is one into which the statements of Acts fit perfectly.

The accuracy which Luke shows in the details we have already examined extends also to the more general sphere of local colour and atmosphere. He gets the atmosphere right every time. Jerusalem, with its excitable and intolerant crowds, is in marked contrast to the busy emporium of Syrian Antioch, where men of different creeds and nationalities rub shoulders and get their rough corners worn away, so that we are not surprised to find the first Gentile church established

[1] See Ramsay, *The Bearing of Recent Discovery*, etc., pp. 297 ff.
[2] *Ursprung und Anfänge des Christentums* i (1921), p. 49.

there, with Jews and non-Jews meeting in brotherly tolerance and fellowship.[1] Then there is Philippi, the Roman colony with its self-important magistrates and its citizens so very proud of being Romans; and Athens, with its endless disputations in the market-place and its unquenchable thirst for the latest news—a thirst for which its statesmen had chided it three and four hundred years earlier.[2] Then there is Ephesus, with its temple of Artemis, one of the seven wonders of the world, and so many of its citizens depending for their living on the cult of the great goddess; with its reputation for superstition and magic—a reputation so widespread in the ancient world that a common name for written charms or spells was *Ephesia grammata* ('Ephesian letters'). It was no doubt scrolls containing these spells that were publicly burnt as Paul powerfully proclaimed a faith which set men free from superstitious fears (Acts xix. 19).

Three sections of the Acts are commonly known as 'we-sections', because in them the writer suddenly passes from a narrative in the third person to one in the first person plural, thus unobtrusively but adequately indicating that at certain periods he himself was present at the events described.[3] Of these 'we-sections' perhaps the most interesting is the last, which contains the great story of Paul's voyage and shipwreck as he and his companions sailed from Palestine to Italy. This narrative has been called 'one of the most instructive documents for the knowledge of ancient seamanship'.[4] The standard work in English on the subject is *The Voyage and Shipwreck of St. Paul,* published in 1848 (4th ed., 1880), by James Smith of Jordanhill, himself an experienced yachtsman who was well acquainted with that part of the Mediterranean over which Paul's ship sailed, and who bears witness to the remarkable accuracy of Luke's account of each stage in the voyage, and was able to fix,

---

[1] Acts xi. 19 ff.
[2] Acts xvii. 21; *cf*. Thucydides iii. 38. 5; Demosthenes, *Philippic* 10.
[3] Acts xvi. 10-17, xx. 5-xxi. 18, xxvii. 1-xxviii. 16.
[4] H. J. Holtzmann, *Handcommentar zum N.T.* (1889), p. 421.

by the details given by Luke, the exact spot on the coast of Malta where the shipwreck must have taken place.

Of Luke's narrative of their stay in Malta (Acts xxviii. 1-10), Harnack says 'that it may be concluded with great probability from xxviii. 9 f. that the author himself practised in Malta as a physician', and after an examination of the language of the passage he declares that 'the whole story of the abode of the narrator in Malta is displayed in a medical light'.[1]

Now, all these evidences of accuracy are not accidental. A man whose accuracy can be demonstrated in matters where we are able to test it is likely to be accurate even where the means for testing him are not available. Accuracy is a habit of mind, and we know from happy (or unhappy) experience that some people are habitually accurate just as others can be depended upon to be inaccurate. Luke's record entitles him to be regarded as a writer of habitual accuracy.

Sir William Ramsay, who devoted many fruitful years to the archæology of Asia Minor, testifies to Luke's intimate and accurate acquaintance with Asia Minor and the Greek East at the time with which his writings deal. When Ramsay first set out on his archæological work, in the late 'seventies of last century, he was firmly convinced of the truth of the then fashionable Tübingen theory, that Acts was a late production of the middle of the second century AD, and he was only gradually compelled to a complete reversal of his views by the inescapable evidence of the facts uncovered in the course of his research.

Although in his later years Ramsay was persuaded to don the mantle of a popular apologist for the trustworthiness of the New Testament records, the judgments which he publicized in this way were judgments which he had previously formed as a scientific archæologist and student of ancient classical history and literature. He was not talking unadvisedly or playing to the religious gallery when he expressed the view that 'Luke's history is unsurpassed in respect of its trustworthiness'[2]; this was

[1] *The Bearing of Recent Discovery*, etc., p. 81.
[2] *Luke the Physician*, pp. 177-179.

the sober conclusion to which his researches led him, in spite of the fact that he started with a very different opinion of Luke's historical credit. His mature verdict was pronounced in the following terms :

'Luke is a historian of the first rank; not merely are his statements of fact trustworthy; he is possessed of the true historic sense; he fixes his mind on the idea and plan that rules in the evolution of history, and proportions the scale of his treatment to the importance of each incident. He seizes the important and critical events and shows their true nature at greater length, while he touches lightly or omits entirely much that was valueless for his purpose. In short, this author should be placed along with the very greatest of historians.'[1]

It is not every scholar who would endorse Ramsay's judgment on Luke's technical expertise as a historian; but his detailed accuracy is something which can be checked time and again. Research in the field which forms the historical and geographical background to Luke's narrative has not stood still since Ramsay's hey-day, but our respect for Luke's reliability continues to grow as our knowledge of this field increases. Whatever may be said of Ramsay, no-one will be inclined to charge the veteran American scholar Dr. Henry J. Cadbury with being an apologist. But when Dr. Cadbury, after a long and distinguished career in which he made contributions of the highest quality to the study of Luke and Acts, delivered the Lowell Lectures for 1953 on *The Book of Acts in History,* he produced a fascinating work which can but enhance the reader's admiration for Luke's achievement. Dr. Cadbury's volume may indeed be hailed as a worthy sequel to Ramsay at his best.

The historical trustworthiness of Luke has indeed been acknowledged by many biblical critics whose standpoint has been definitely liberal. And it is a conclusion of high importance for those who consider the New Testament from the angle of the historian. For

[1] *Bearing,* p. 222. Compare the verdict of the Emeritus Professor of Classics in Auckland University, New Zealand: 'Luke is a consummate historian, to be ranged in his own right with the great writers of the Greeks' (E. M. Blaiklock, *The Acts of the Apostles* [Tyndale Press, 1959], p. 89).

the writings of Luke cover the period of our Lord's life and death, and the first thirty years of the Christian Church, including the years in which Paul's greatest missionary work was accomplished and the majority of his extant letters were written. The two parts of Luke's history really bind the New Testament together, his Gospel dealing with the same events as the other Gospels, and his Acts providing the historical background to the Epistles of Paul. The picture which Luke gives us of the rise of Christianity is generally consonant with the witness of the other three Gospels and of Paul's letters. And he puts this picture in the frame of contemporary history in a way which would inevitably invite exposure if his work were that of a romancer, but which in fact provides a test and vindication on historical grounds of the trustworthiness of his own writings, and with them or at least the main outline of the origins of Christianity presented to us in the New Testament as a whole.[1]

[1] See I. H. Marshall, *Luke: Historian and Theologian* (1970).

CHAPTER 8

MORE ARCHAEOLOGICAL EVIDENCE

THE archæological evidence bearing on the New Testament is not so imposing as that bearing on the Old Testament; but, though less spectacular, it is not less important. We have already considered some of the evidence from inscriptions and papyri; we may look at one or two more examples before passing on to evidence of another kind.

The reader of Acts will remember that on Paul's last visit to Jerusalem, a riot arose in the temple because the rumour got around that he had polluted the sacred precincts by taking Gentiles into them.[1] Gentiles might enter the outer court, which was not really part of the temple buildings proper; but they might not penetrate farther on pain of death.[2] So anxious were the Roman authorities to conciliate the religious susceptibilities of the Jews that they even sanctioned the execution of Roman citizens for this offence.[3] That none might plead ignorance of the rule, notices in Greek and Latin were fastened to the barricade separating the outer from the inner courts, warning Gentiles that death was the penalty for trespass. One of these Greek inscriptions, found at Jerusalem in 1871 by C. S. Clermont-Ganneau, is now housed in Istanbul, and reads as follows :

NO FOREIGNER MAY ENTER WITHIN THE BARRICADE WHICH SURROUNDS THE TEMPLE AND ENCLOSURE. ANYONE WHO IS CAUGHT DOING SO WILL HAVE HIMSELF TO THANK FOR HIS ENSUING DEATH.[4]

When Paul wrote in Ephesians ii. 14 of 'the middle

[1] Acts xxi. 27 ff.
[2] Josephus, *Jewish War* v. 5. 2.
[3] *Ibid.* vi. 2. 4.
[4] Another, but imperfect, copy was found at Jerusalem some sixty years later; it is in the Rockefeller Museum in Jerusalem.

wall of partition' between Jew and Gentile which is broken down in Christ, it has been thought that his metaphor was drawn from this temple barrier, which forbade Gentiles to trespass on ground reserved for Jews alone.

Other New Testament incidents have been illuminated by archæological discoveries in and around Jerusalem. The pool of Bethesda, described in John v. 2, has been located in the north-east quarter of the old city of Jerusalem, the quarter which was called Bezetha, or 'New Town', in the first century AD. In 1888 excavations near St. Anne's Church, in that quarter, revealed the remains of an ancient church building, clearly intended to mark the site of Bethesda. Later excavations have identified the pool itself, or rather twin pools, lying north and south, with a rock partition between them. Porticoes evidently occupied the four sides and the partition.[1] One of the first visitors to Jerusalem after it came under Christian control, the 'Bordeaux pilgrim' (AD 333), saw and described the twin pools. The 'Copper Scroll' from Qumran gives the name in the Hebrew dual number, *Beth-'esh-dathain*, 'the place of the two outpourings'. There are few sites in Jerusalem, mentioned in the Gospels, which can be identified so confidently.

The identification of New Testament sites in Jerusalem can rarely be made with such confidence because of the destruction of the city in AD 70 and the founding of a new pagan city on the site in AD 135. Besides, it is not practicable to conduct archæological excavations on any scale in a city which is still so densely populated. Hence, for example, there is still some doubt about the place where our Lord was crucified and buried. The traditional site, occupied by the Church of the Holy Sepulchre, is that which was pointed out to the Emperor Constantine when he visited Jerusalem in AD 327, and it is now certain that it lay outside the 'second wall' of Jerusalem, as Golgotha must have done. The course of this wall has not yet been fully traced.[2]

[1] *Cf.* J. Jeremias, *The Rediscovery of Bethesda* (1966).

[2] *Cf.* K. M. Kenyon, *Jerusalem: Excavating* 3000 *Years of History* (1967), pp. 146 ff.

In 1945 the late Professor E. L. Sukenik of the Hebrew University found what he claimed to be 'the earliest records of Christianity' in inscriptions written on two ossuaries or repositories for human bones near Jerusalem. But it now seems fairly certain that the inscriptions have nothing to do with Christianity, but refer to two separate first-century individuals named Jesus, neither of them being Jesus of Nazareth.[1]

Writing his Epistle to the Romans from Corinth during the winter of AD 56-57, Paul sends greetings from some of his companions, and adds : 'Erastus the City Treasurer greets you' (Rom. xvi. 23). In the course of excavations in Corinth in 1929, Professor T. L. Shear found a pavement with the inscription ERASTVS PRO : AED : S :P : STRAVIT ('Erastus, curator of public buildings, laid this pavement at his own expense'). The evidence indicates that this pavement existed in the first century AD, and it is most probable that the donor is identical with the Erastus who is mentioned by Paul.

From Corinth, too, we have a fragmentary inscription which originally stood over a doorway; when complete, it appears to have said 'Synagogue of the Hebrews'. Conceivably it belonged to the synagogue in which Paul debated when he came to Corinth, until the authorities could no longer tolerate his activity and he had to move next door, to the house of Justus (Acts xviii. 4-7). Yet another Corinthian inscription identifies the *makellon* or 'meat market' of the city, to which Paul refers in 1 Corinthians x. 25 (AV 'shambles').

Sometimes minor details in the New Testament narrative have been illuminated and confirmed by archæological research. For example, when Paul and Barnabas, in the course of their first missionary tour, visited Lystra in Asia Minor, and healed a lame man, the populace jumped to the conclusion that the gods had come down to them in the likeness of men, 'and they called Barnabas Zeus, and Paul Hermes, because he was the chief speaker' (Acts xiv. 12). Now Zeus and Hermes (whom the Romans called Jupiter and Mercury) were tradi-

[1] *Cf.* J. P. Kane, 'By No Means "The Earliest Records of Christianity" ', *Palestine Exploration Quarterly* ciii (1971), pp. 103 ff.

tionally connected with that region; in the eighth book of his *Metamorphoses* (lines 626 ff.) the poet Ovid tells a well-known story of how they came to those parts incognito and received hospitality from an aged couple, Philemon and Baucis, who were well rewarded for their kindness, while their inhospitable neighbours were over-whelmed by a deluge.

But more precise evidence of the joint worship of these two deities in the vicinity of Lystra was found in 1910, when Sir William Calder discovered an inscription of *c.* AD 250 at Sedasa near Lystra, recording the dedica-tion to Zeus of a statue of Hermes along with a sundial by men with Lycaonian names,[1] and again in 1926, when the same scholar, along with Professor W. H. Buckler, discovered a stone altar near Lystra dedicated to the 'Hearer of Prayer' (presumably Zeus) and Hermes.[2]

A good parallel to the phrase 'the chief speaker' (Gk., *ho hēgoumenos tou logou*; literally, 'the leader of the speaking') is found in *The Egyptian Mysteries* of Iamblichus, where Hermes is described as 'the god who is the leader of the speeches' (Gk., *theos ho tōn logōn hēgemōn*). In their way, these 'undesigned coincidences' are as telling as the more direct confirmations of biblical statements.

We have already seen something of the importance of papyrus discoveries for New Testament studies, when discussing some early fragments of Scripture that have been found among them.[3] But these by no means exhaust the interest which these papyrus finds have for us. One of the happiest consequences of these discoveries has been the coming to light of a great quantity of Greek writing on scraps of papyrus (or on pieces of pottery) by people of little education, and we are thus able to see the sort of Greek spoken by the common people of New Testament times—at any rate in Egypt.

Now, it had always been recognized that the Greek

---

[1] See *Classical Review* xxiv (1910), pp. 79 ff., xxxviii (1924), p. 29, n. 1; *Expositor*, July, 1910, pp. 1 ff., 148 ff.
[2] See *Discovery* vii (1926), p. 262.
[3] See pp. 17 ff.

of the New Testament was different in many ways from the classical language of the great Greek writers. Scholars tried to account for the peculiarities of this 'biblical Greek' in various ways; some, like Richard Rothe in 1863, suggested that it was a new 'language of the Holy Ghost',[1] invented for the purpose of expressing divine truth. We do not, of course, deny that, in whatever language the New Testament was written, it would certainly be in one sense 'a language of the Holy Ghost', when we consider the good news and divine truth conveyed to us in that language; but the discovery of these unliterary writings in the sands of Egypt quite reversed the previous opinions of scholars, for they turned out to be written in much the same kind of Greek as the New Testament. The Greek of the New Testament, in fact, was very like the vernacular *Koine* or 'common' Greek of the day; the 'language of the Holy Ghost' was found to be the language of the common people—a lesson which we should do well to keep in mind.[2]

Great excitement was aroused towards the end of last century and the beginning of this one by the discovery by B. P. Grenfell and A. S. Hunt at Oxyrhynchus of three papyrus fragments containing sayings of Jesus, some of which were similar to sayings occurring in our Gospels, while others had no known parallels. The discovery of otherwise unknown sayings of Jesus is not surprising; in the early days of the Church a great number of them must have been current, transmitted from one generation to another. These Oxyrhynchus papyri, which were dated not later than AD 140, were

[1] Quoted by H. Cremer in the Preface to his *Biblico-Theologica Lexicon of New Testament Greek*.

[2] We should not, however, exaggerate this similarity between New Testament Greek and the vernacular of the papyri, the former being a more literary dialect. To quote Professor A. D. Nock, 'Any man who knows his classical Greek authors and reads the New Testament and then looks into the papyri is astonished at the similarities which he finds. Any man who knows the papyri first and then turns to Paul is astonished at the differences. There has been much exaggeration of the Koine element in the New Testament' (*Journal of Biblical Literature* lii [1933], p. 138). See also E. K. Simpson, *Words Worth Weighing in the Greek New Testament* (Tyndale Press, 1944). But in general the above account is true.

not fragments of a Gospel, like the papyri mentioned in an earlier chapter; they had formed part of collections of isolated sayings, each introduced by such words as 'Jesus said'. Whether they are all genuine sayings of Jesus is doubtful. But it is interesting that some of them represent Jesus as speaking in the way in which He speaks in the fourth Gospel, though the resemblance is one of subject-matter rather than style.

In 1946 there was discovered in Egypt a Coptic version of a work (originally composed in Greek) called the 'Gospel of Thomas', which consists of 114 sayings of Jesus, strung together without narrative framework. Among them are found those previously known from the three Oxyrhynchus papyri. The collection opens with the words :

'These are the secret words which the living Jesus spoke and Didymus Judas Thomas wrote them down, and he said: "Whosoever finds the interpretation of these words shall not taste death."[1] Jesus said: "Let not him who seeks cease to seek until he finds, and when he finds he will be stirred; when he is stirred he will marvel, and he will reign over the universe." '[2]

The relation of these sayings to the canonical tradition must be a matter for further study. It is evident that several of them reflect a Gnostic outlook.

The Gnostic colouring of this 'Gospel of Thomas' is not surprising, because it was found along with a whole library of Gnostic texts. These texts, called the Nag Hammadi texts from the name of the place where they were discovered (the ancient Chenoboskion, on the west bank of the Nile some sixty miles north of Luxor), comprise forty-nine treatises in thirteen papyrus codices. The codices belong to the third and fourth centuries AD, but the Greek originals were composed a century or two earlier. They do not help us to understand the New Testament better, although they do show us what was thought of its meaning by a very significant, if unortho-

---

[1] *Cf.* Jn. viii. 51.
[2] This last saying ('Let not him who seeks . . .') is quoted, with variations, by Clement of Alexandria (*c.* AD 180) as coming from the Gospel according to the Hebrews (see pp. 25, 27 f.).

dox, body of people in the second century; and they show that orthodox churchmen were not the only ones who accepted practically the whole catholic canon of New Testament writings as early as the middle of that century.

Reference has already been made to the affinities in thought and language traced between the Qumran documents and the Gospel of John. These documents, which have come to light since 1947, tell us much about the life and faith of a Jewish community which flourished for about 200 years (*c.* 130 BC–AD 70) and which resembled the primitive Christian community in a number of respects. Both communities regarded themselves as the true remnant of Israel, both supported this claim by a distinctive interpretation of the Old Testament, and both interpreted their calling in eschatological terms. Whether direct contact can be established between the two communities is doubtful; thus far the least unpromising attempts to do so have centred round the figure of John the Baptist. Alongside the resemblances between the two communities, we must take note of some radical differences, and chief among these is the fact that primitive Christianity was dominated by the uniqueness of Jesus' person and work, and by the consciousness of being energized by His risen power. But these discoveries have begun to fill in a hitherto blank area in the setting of the gospel story, and will no doubt continue to illuminate New Testament studies in exciting and unexpected ways.[1]

[1] *Cf.* K. Stendahl (ed.), *The Scrolls and the New Testament* (1957); F. F. Bruce, 'The Dead Sea Scrolls and Early Christianity', *Bulletin of the John Rylands Library* xlix (1966-67), pp. 69 ff.; G. Vermes, *The Dead Sea Scrolls: Qumran in Perspective* (1977).

CHAPTER 9

THE EVIDENCE OF
EARLY JEWISH WRITINGS

1. *The Rabbinical Writings*

WHEN the city of Jerusalem fell in AD 70, together with the temple, the dominion of the priestly families and the supreme court of the Sanhedrin fell with them. The only party in Judaism which was capable of undertaking the necessary work of reconstruction was that of the Pharisees, and this they did, not on a political but on a spiritual basis. Led by Yohanan the son of Zakkai, they made their headquarters at Jabneh or Jamnia, in the south-west of Palestine. Here they reconstituted the Sanhedrin as a supreme court for the organization of the whole range of religious law, with Yohanan as its first president in its new form. A great body of case-law, 'the tradition of the elders' mentioned in the New Testament, had been handed down orally from generation to generation, increasing with the years. The first step towards codifying all this material was now taken. The second step was taken by the great Rabbi Akiba, who was the first to arrange it according to subject-matter. After his heroic death in AD 135, on the defeat of Bar-Kokhba's rebellion against Rome, his work was revised and continued by his pupil Rabbi Meir. The work of codification was brought to completion about AD 200 by Rabbi Judah, president of the Sanhedrin from 170 to 217. The whole code of religious jurisprudence thus compiled is known as the Mishnah.

This completed Mishnah itself became an object of study, and a body of commentary grew up around it in the rabbinical schools both of Palestine and of Babylonia. These commentaries or Gemaras formed a sort of supplement to the Mishnah, and Mishnah and Gemara together are usually known as the Talmud. The

'Jerusalem Talmud', consisting of the Mishnah together with the accumulated Gemara of the Palestinian schools, was completed about AD 300; the much larger Babylonian Talmud continued to grow for two centuries more, before it was reduced to writing about the year 500.

As the Mishnah is a law-code, and the Talmuds commentaries on this code, there is little occasion in these writings for references to Christianity, and what references there are are hostile. But, such as they are, these references do at least show that there was not the slightest doubt of the historical character of Jesus.[1]

According to the earlier Rabbis whose opinions are recorded in these writings, Jesus of Nazareth was a transgressor in Israel, who practised magic, scorned the words of the wise, led the people astray, and said he had not come to destroy the law but to add to it.[2] He was hanged on Passover Eve for heresy and misleading the people. His disciples, of whom five are named, healed the sick in his name.

It is clear that this is just such a portrayal of our Lord as we might expect from those elements in the Pharisaic party which were opposed to Him. Some of the names by which He is called bear witness directly or indirectly to the Gospel record. The appellation *Ha-Taluy* ('The Hanged One') obviously refers to the manner of His death; another name given to Him, *Ben-Pantera* ('Son of Pantera'), probably refers, not (as has sometimes been alleged) to a Roman soldier named Pantheras, but to the Christian belief in our Lord's virgin birth, *Pantera* being a corruption of the Greek *parthenos* ('virgin').[3] This does not mean, of course, that all those who called Him by this name *believed* in His virgin birth.

About the end of the first century AD and beginning of the second, there seems to have been a controversy in some Jewish circles as to whether some Christian writings should be recognized as canonical or not. These

[1] See J. Klausner, *Jesus of Nazareth* (1929), pp. 18 ff.; M. Goguel, *Life of Jesus* (1933), pp. 70 ff.
[2] *Cf.* Mt. v. 17.
[3] See Klausner, *Jesus of Nazareth*, pp. 23 f.

writings, whatever they were, went by the name *Euangelion,* the Greek word for 'Gospel'. The *Euangelion* in question was most probably an Aramaic form of the Gospel according to Matthew, the favourite Gospel of the Jewish Christians in Palestine and the adjoining territory. Rabbi Yohanan and Rabbi Meir are said to have made unfriendly puns on the word *Euangelion* by altering its vowels to make it read *'Awen-gillayon* or *'Awon-gillayon,* meaning something like 'Iniquity of the Margin' or 'Sin of the Writing-tablet'.[1] These obscure references indicate that there was some contact between the orthodox Pharisees and the Jewish Christians, which is not surprising if we remember that according to the New Testament the early Palestinian church included believing members of the Pharisaic party and several thousand Jews who were 'all zealots for the law' (Acts xv. 5, xxi. 20). After AD 70, indeed, these Jewish Christians may have had more contact with other Jews than with members of the Gentile churches, who were increasingly inclined to write off the Jewish Christian communities as heretical and sub-Christian. In particular, there are grounds for thinking that those refugees from the Jerusalem church who settled in Transjordan about the year 70 made common cause with certain Essene groups, possibly including the remnants of the Qumran community.

2. *Josephus*

But we have earlier and more important Jewish literature for our purpose than anything found in the Talmuds. The Jewish historian Josephus was born of a priestly family in AD 37. At the age of nineteen he joined the Pharisaic party. On a visit to Rome in AD 63 he was able to take stock of the might of the Empire. On the outbreak of the Jewish War in AD 66 he was made commander of the Jewish forces in Galilee, and defended the stronghold of Jotapata against the Romans until further resistance was useless. He then escaped to a cave with forty others, and when this new refuge seemed likely to be taken they arranged a suicide pact. Perhaps

[1] Babylonian Talmud, tractate *Shabbath,* 116 a, b.

more by good management than by good luck Josephus found himself one of the last two survivors. He persuaded his fellow-survivor that they might as well give themselves up to the Romans, and when they had done so he contrived to win the favour of Vespasian, the Roman commander, by predicting his elevation to the imperial purple, a prediction which was fulfilled in AD 69. Josephus was attached to the Roman general headquarters during the siege of Jerusalem, even acting as interpreter for Titus, Vespasian's son and successor in the Palestinian command, when he wished to make proclamation to the beleaguered inhabitants. After the fall of the city and crushing of the rebellion, Josephus settled down comfortably in Rome as a client and pensioner of the emperor, whose family name Flavius he assumed, being thenceforth known as Flavius Josephus.

Naturally, this variegated career did not tend to make him popular with his fellow-countrymen, many of whom did—and still do—look on him as a double-dyed traitor. However, he employed his years of leisure in Rome in such a way as to establish some claim upon their gratitude, by writing the history of their nation. His literary works include a *History of the Jewish War*, from 170 BC to AD 73, written first in Aramaic for the benefit of the Jews on the easternmost confines of the Empire, and then published in a Greek version; an *Autobiography*, in which he defends his conduct against another Jewish historian, Justus of Tiberias, who in his account of the war had taken a poor view of the part played by Josephus; two books *Against Apion*, in which he defends his nation against the anti-Semitic calumnies (some of which sound quite modern) of Apion, an Alexandrian schoolmaster, and other writers; and twenty books of *Antiquities of the Jews*, recording the history of his nation from the beginning of Genesis down to his own day. However little he may have deserved to survive the downfall of his nation, we may well be glad that he did survive, for without his historical works, in spite of all their imperfections, we should be almost incredibly poorer in sources of information about the history of Palestine in New Testament times.

Here, in the pages of Josephus, we meet many figures who are well known to us from the New Testament : the colourful family of the Herods; the Roman emperors Augustus, Tiberius, Claudius, and Nero; Quirinius, the governor of Syria; Pilate, Felix, and Festus, the procurators of Judæa; the high-priestly families—Annas, Caiaphas, Ananias, and the rest; the Pharisees and Sadducees; and so on. Against the background which Josephus provides we can read the New Testament with greater understanding and interest.

When Gamaliel, in Acts v. 37, speaks of Judas the Galilæan who led a rising in the days of the taxing, we turn to the pages of Josephus, and find the story of this rising both in his *War* (ii. 8) and in the *Antiquities* (xviii. 1). Josephus also tells of an impostor named Theudas (*Ant.* xx. 5. 1) who appeared shortly after AD 44, but the Theudas mentioned by Gamaliel flourished before Judas the Galilæan (AD 6), and in any case Gamaliel's speech was made between 30 and 33. It is unnecessary to think that Luke perpetrated an anachronism through misreading Josephus (the weight of evidence is against Luke's having read Josephus); Josephus himself tells us that about the time of the death of Herod the Great (4 BC) there were ever so many such troubles in Judæa,[1] and the activity of Gamaliel's Theudas (which was not an uncommon name) may belong to this period.

The famine in the days of Claudius (Acts xi. 28) is also referred to by Josephus; if Luke tells us how the Christians in Antioch sent help to the Jerusalem church on this occasion, Josephus tells us how Helena, the Jewish queen-mother of Adiabene, which lay north-east of Mesopotamia, had corn bought in Alexandria and figs in Cyprus to relieve the hunger of the Jerusalem populace on the same occasion.[2]

The sudden death of Herod Agrippa I, narrated by Luke in Acts xii. 19-23, is recorded also by Josephus

[1] *Ant.* xvii. 10. 4.
[2] *Ant.* xx .2 . 5.

(*Ant.* xix. 8. 2) in a form agreeing with Luke's general outline, though the two accounts are quite independent of each other. This is the story as told by Josephus :

· 'When Agrippa had reigned three full years over all Judæa, he came to the city of Cæsarea, which was formerly called Strato's Tower. There he exhibited shows in honour of Cæsar, inaugurating this as a festival for the emperor's welfare.[1] And there came together to it a multitude of the provincial officials and of those who had been promoted to a distinguished position. On the second day of the shows he put on a robe all made of silver, of altogether wonderful weaving, and arrived in the theatre at break of day. Then the silver shone as the sun's first rays fell upon it and glittered wonderfully, its resplendence inspiring a sort of fear and trembling in those who gazed upon it. Immediately his flatterers called out from various quarters, in words which in truth were not for his good, addressing him as a god, and invoking him with the cry, "Be propitious! if hitherto we have revered thee as a human being, yet henceforth we confess thee to be superior to mortal nature."

'The king did not rebuke them, nor did he repudiate their impious flattery. But looking up soon afterwards he saw the owl sitting on a rope above his head, and immediately recognized it as a messenger of evil as it had formerly been a messenger of good,[2] and a pang of grief pierced his heart. There came also a severe pain in his belly, beginning with a violent attack. . . . So he was carried quickly into the palace, and the news sped abroad among all that he would certainly die before long. . . . And when he had suffered continuously for five days from the pain in his belly, he departed this life in the fifty-fourth year of his age and the seventh of his reign.'

The parallels between the two accounts are obvious, as is also the absence of collusion between them. Luke describes the king's sudden stroke by saying, in biblical language, that 'the angel of the Lord smote him'; it is unnecessary to think that there is any significance in the

---

[1] Possibly on Claudius' birthday, which fell on 1 August.

[2] When he had been cast into bonds by order of the Emperor Tiberius several years previously, he leaned against a tree upon which sat an owl; and a German fellow-prisoner told him that the bird betokened a speedy deliverance for him and an accession of good fortune, but that if ever he saw it again he would have but five days longer to live (*Ant.* xviii. 6. 7.).

fact that the Greek word for 'angel' in Luke's account (*angelos*) is the same as the word for 'messenger' applied to the owl by Josephus, though some early Christian Fathers seem to have thought so. The Tyrians may well have taken advantage of this festival to be publicly reconciled to the king.

In general, we may sum up the comparison of the two accounts in the words of an unbiased historian, Eduard Meyer : 'In outline, in data, and in the general conception, both accounts are in full agreement. By its very interesting details, which are by no means to be explained as due to a "tendency" or a popular tradition, Luke's account affords a guarantee that it is at least just as reliable as that of Josephus.'[1]

More important still, Josephus makes mention of John the Baptist and of James the brother of our Lord, recording the death of each in a manner manifestly independent of the New Testament, so that there is no ground for suspecting Christian interpolation in either passage. In *Ant*. xviii. 5. 2 we read how Herod Antipas, the tetrarch of Galilee, was defeated in battle by Aretas, king of the Nabatæan Arabs, the father of Herod's first wife, whom he deserted for Herodias. Josephus goes on :

'Now some of the Jews thought that Herod's army had been destroyed by God, and that it was a very just penalty to avenge John, surnamed the Baptist. For Herod had killed him, though he was a good man, who bade the Jews practise virtue, be just one to another and pious toward God, and come together in baptism.[2] He taught that baptism was acceptable to God provided that they underwent it not to procure remission of certain sins, but for the purification of the body, if the soul had already been purified by righteousness. And when the others gathered round him (for they were greatly moved when they heard his words), Herod feared that his persuasive power over men, being so great, might lead to a rising, as they seemed ready to follow his counsel in everything. So he thought it much better to seize him and kill him before he caused any tumult, than to have to repent of falling into such trouble

---

[1] *Ursprung und Anfänge des Christentums* iii (1923), pp. 167 f.
[2] This seems to envisage the formation of a religious community which was entered by baptism.

later on, after a revolt had taken place. Because of this suspicion of Herod, John was sent in chains to Machærus, the fortress which we mentioned above, and there put to death. The Jews believed that it was to avenge him that the disaster fell upon the army, God wishing to bring evil upon Herod.'

There are striking differences between this and the Gospel account: according to Mark i. 4, John 'proclaimed a baptism of repentance for remission of sins', whereas Josephus says that John's baptism was not for the remission of sins; and the story of John's death is given a political significance by Josephus, whereas in the Gospels it resulted from John's denunciation of Herod's marriage to Herodias. It is quite likely that Herod thought he could kill two birds with one stone by imprisoning John; and as for the discrepancy about the significance of John's baptism, the independent traditions which we can trace in the New Testament are impressively unanimous, and besides being earlier than the account in Josephus (the *Antiquities* were published in AD 93), they give what is a more probable account from the religious-historical point of view. Josephus, in fact, seems to attribute to John the baptismal doctrine of the Essenes, as known to us now from the Qumran texts. But the general outline of the story in Josephus confirms the Gospel record. The Josephus passage was known to Origen (*c.* AD 230) and to Eusebius (*c.* AD 326).[1]

Later in the *Antiquities* (xx. 9. 1), Josephus describes the high-handed acts of the high priest Ananus after the death of the procurator Festus (AD 61) in these words:

'But the younger Ananus who, as we said, received the high priesthood, was of a bold disposition and exceptionally daring; he followed the party of the Sadducees, who are severe in judgment above all the Jews, as we have already shown. As therefore Ananus was of such a disposition, he thought he had now a good opportunity, as Festus was now dead, and Albinus was still on the road; so he assembled a council of judges, and brought before it the brother of Jesus the so-called Christ, whose name was James, together with some others, and having accused them as law-breakers, he delivered them over to be stoned.'

[1] Origen, *Contra Celsum* i. 47; Eusebius, *H.E.* i. 11.

This passage, like the previous one, was also known to Origen and Eusebius.[1] The story of the death of James the Just (as the Lord's brother was called) is told in greater detail by Hegesippus, a Jewish Christian writer of *c.* AD 170.[2] The account in Josephus is chiefly important because he calls James 'the brother of Jesus the so-called Christ', in such a way as to suggest that he has already made some reference to Jesus. And we do find a reference to Him in all extant copies of Josephus, the so-called *Testimonium Flavianum* in *Antiquities* xviii. 3. 3. There Josephus narrates some of the troubles which marked the procuratorship of Pilate, and continues :

'And there arose about this time Jesus, a wise man, *if indeed we should call him a man;* for he was a doer of marvellous deeds, a teacher of men who receive the truth with pleasure. He led away many Jews, and also many of the Greeks. *This man was the Christ.* And when Pilate had condemned him to the cross on his impeachment by the chief men among us, those who had loved him at first did not cease; *for he appeared to them on the third day alive again, the divine prophets having spoken these and thousands of other wonderful things about him:* and even now the tribe of Christians, so named after him, has not yet died out.'

This is a translation of the text of this passage as it has come down to us, and we know that it was the same in the time of Eusebius, who quotes it twice.[3] One reason why many have decided to regard it as a Christian interpolation is that Origen says that Josephus did not believe Jesus to be the Messiah nor proclaim Him as such.[4] That Josephus was no Christian is certain in any case. But it seems unlikely that a writer who was not a Christian should use the expressions printed above in italics. Yet there is nothing to say against the passage on the ground of textual criticism; the manuscript evidence is as unanimous and ample as it is for anything in Josephus. It may be, however, that Origen knew the

[1] Origen, *Contra Celsum* i. 47; ii. 13; *Comm. in Matt.* x. 17; Eusebius, *H.E.* ii. 23.

[2] The narrative of Hegesippus is preserved in Eusebius, *H.E.* ii. 23.

[3] *H.E.* i. 11; *Demonstratio Evangelica* iii. 5.

[4] *Contra Celsum* i. 47; *Comm. in Matt.* x. 17.

passage in an earlier form, which lacked the italicized sections.[1] Since the text of Josephus has been transmitted by Christians and not by Jews, it is not surprising if his reference to Jesus should have acquired a more Christian flavour in the course of time.

If, however, we look more closely at these italicized sections, it may occur to us to wonder if it is not possible that Josephus was writing with his tongue in his cheek. *'If indeed we should call him a man'* may be a sarcastic reference to the Christians' belief in Jesus as the Son of God. *'This man was the Christ'* may mean no more than that this was the Jesus commonly called the Christ. Some such reference is in any case implied by the later statement that the Christians were called after Him. As for the third italicized section, the one about the resurrection, this may simply be intended to record what the Christians averred. Some acute critics have found no difficulty in accepting the *Testimonium Flavianum* as it stands.[2] The passage certainly contains several characteristic features of the diction of Josephus, as has been pointed out by the late Dr. H. St. John Thackeray (the leading British authority on Josephus in recent years)[3] and others.

It has also been pointed out that omission of words and short phrases is characteristic of the textual tradition of the *Antiquities*,[4] which makes it easier to accept a suggestion that the word 'so-called' has dropped out before 'Christ', and some such phrase as 'as they said' or possibly 'as they say' after 'for he appeared to them'.[5] Both these suggested emendations are attractive, the former especially so, because the very phrase 'the so-

---

[1] *Cf.* T. Reinach, 'Josèphe sur Jésus', *Revue des Études juives* xxxv (1897), pp. 13 f.; J. Klausner, *Jesus of Nazareth*, pp. 55 ff. Klausner accepts the passage as genuine apart from the sections italicized above; this verdict by so distinguished a Jewish authority on the history of the second temple is worthy of respect.

[2] *Cf.* F. C. Burkitt, *The Gospel History and its Transmission* (1906), p. 325.

[3] *Josephus, the Man and the Historian* (1929), pp. 125 ff.

[4] *Cf.* G. C. Richards, in *Journal of Theological Studies* xlii (1941), pp. 70 f.

[5] *Cf.* R. J. H. Shutt, in *Classical Quarterly* xxxi (1937), p. 176

called Christ' occurs in the passage where Josephus related the death of James.

Two other emendations have much to commend them. One is a suggestion of Thackeray, that instead of 'the truth' (Greek *alēthē*) we should read 'strange things' (Greek *aēthē*). The other is a suggestion of Dr. Robert Eisler, that some words have fallen out at the beginning of the passage, which originally commenced : 'And there arose about this time a source of new troubles, one Jesus.' If, then, we adopt these emendations of the text, this is what we get as a result :

'And there arose about this time *a source of new troubles*,[1] one Jesus, a wise man. He was a doer of marvellous deeds, a teacher of men who receive *strange things* with pleasure. He led away many Jews, and also many of the Greeks. This man was the *so-called* Christ. And when Pilate had condemned him to the cross on his impeachment by the chief men among us, those who had loved him at first did not cease; for he appeared to them, *as they said*, on the third day alive again, the divine prophets having spoken these and thousands of other wonderful things about him: and even now the tribe of Christians, so named after him, has not yet died out.'

The italics this time mark the emendations. This version of the *Testimonium* has got rid, by one or two

[1] The main difficulty about accepting this emendation of Eisler's, which in itself is probable enough, as it makes the passage fit more naturally into the context, is the wild company it keeps. On the basis of a radically emended text of the *Testimonium Flavianum*, together with a radically emended text of a late interpolation in the Slavonic version of Josephus' *Jewish War*, Dr. Eisler erected a complete reconstruction of the history of Christian beginnings in *The Messiah Jesus and John the Baptist* (1931). His reconstruction, though brilliantly ingenious and fascinating, is quite perverse and unscientific, for it is erected upon texts which he has first altered to fit the theories which he proceeds to deduce from his emendations.

Although the passage in the Slavonic version of the *Jewish War* is generally regarded as a Christian interpolation, Thackeray was inclined to look favourably upon it (see his Loeb *Josephus*, iii, pp. 648 ff.). It is placed in the *Jewish War* between ii. 9. 3 and ii. 9. 4, and runs as follows:

'At that time there appeared a certain man, if it is meet to call him a man. His nature and form were human, but his appearance more than that of a human being; yet his works were divine. He wrought miracles wonderful and mighty. Wherefore it is impossible for me to call him a human being. But, on the other hand, if I look at his nature as shared by others, I will not call him an angel.

'And all, whatsoever he wrought through an invisible power, he wrought by a word and command. Some said of him, "Our first lawgiver is risen from the dead, and has shown forth cures and prodigies." But the others thought that he was sent from God. But in many things he opposed the law and kept not the sabbath according to the custom of our forefathers. Yet again, he did nothing shameful nor did he operate with his hands, but he prepared everything merely by his word. And many of the multitude followed after him and hearkened to his teaching. And many souls were roused, thinking that thereby the Jewish tribes could free themselves from Roman hands. But it was his custom rather to abide without the city on the Mount of Olives. There also he granted cures to the people. And there gathered to him of helpers a hundred and fifty, but of the populace a multitude. But when they saw his power, that he accomplished by a word whatsoever he would, and when they had made known to him their will, that he should enter the city and cut down the Roman troops and Pilate, and rule over them, he did not heed it. And when thereafter news of it was brought to the Jewish leaders, they assembled together with the high priest and said, "We are powerless and too weak to resist the Romans. Since, however, the bow is bent, we will go and communicate to Pilate what we have heard, and we shall be free from trouble, in order that he may not hear it from others and we be robbed of our goods and ourselves slaughtered and our children dispersed." And they went and reported it to Pilate. And he sent and had many of the multitude slain. And he had that wonder-worker brought up, and after he had held an enquiry concerning him, he pronounced this judgment: "He is a benefactor, but not a malefactor nor a rebel nor covetous of kingship." And he let him go, for he had healed his dying wife. And after he had gone to his wonted place, he did his wonted works. And when more people again gathered round him, he glorified himself by his activity more than all. The scribes were stung with envy and gave Pilate thirty talents to kill him. And he took it and gave them liberty to carry out their will. And they took him and crucified him contrary to the law of their fathers.'

Only by merciless mutilation could Eisler turn this passage into one such as a Jewish writer could have penned. The Christian interpolator introduces a few reminiscences from the *Testimonium Flavianum*, but he does his best to minimize the guilt of Pilate and the Romans, and to emphasize that of the Jews.

Other fragments of a Christian nature in the Slavonic version of the *Jewish War* refer to John the Baptist; Philip the tetrarch (*cf.* Lk. iii. 1); the Christians in Palestine in the time of Claudius; an inscription in the temple alleged to commemorate the crucifixion of Jesus because He foretold the fall of the city and temple; the rent veil and the rising of Jesus; and the oracle mentioned in the ordinary edition at vi. 5. 4, that Palestine would produce a world-ruler. A detailed examination of all these Slavonic additions, with a critique of Eisler's theory, is given in J. W. Jack, *The Historic Christ* (1933).

very simple devices, of the difficulties of the traditional text, while it preserves (or even enhances) the worth of the passage as a historical document. The flavour of contempt is a little more marked as a result of the additions; and the closing reference to 'the tribe of Christians' is not inconsonant with a hope that though they have not yet died out, they soon may.

We have therefore very good reason for believing that Josephus did make reference to Jesus, bearing witness to (*a*) His date, (*b*) His reputation as a wonder-worker, (*c*) His being the brother of James, (*d*) His crucifixion under Pilate at the information of the Jewish rulers, (*e*) His messianic claim, (*f*) His being the founder of 'the tribe of Christians' and probably (g) the belief in His rising from the dead.[1]

[1] *Cf.* F. F. Bruce, *Jesus and Christian Origins Outside the New Testament* (1974), pp. 32–65.

CHAPTER 10

THE EVIDENCE OF
EARLY GENTILE WRITERS

SO much, then, for the information we can gather from early Jewish writings; we turn now to the Gentiles.

The first Gentile writer who concerns us seems to be one called Thallus, who about AD 52 wrote a work tracing the history of Greece and its relations with Asia from the Trojan War to his own day.[1] He has been identified with a Samaritan of that name, who is mentioned by Josephus (*Ant.* xviii. 6. 4) as being a freedman of the Emperor Tiberius. Now Julius Africanus, a Christian writer on chronology about AD 221, who knew the writings of Thallus, says when discussing the darkness which fell upon the land during the crucifixion of Christ: 'Thallus, in the third book of his histories, explains away this darkness as an eclipse of the sun—unreasonably, as it seems to me' (unreasonably, of course, because a solar eclipse could not take place at the time of the full moon, and it was at the season of the Paschal full moon that Christ died).[2]

From this reference in Julius Africanus it has been inferred (*a*) that the gospel tradition, or at least the traditional story of the passion, was known in Rome in non-Christian circles towards the middle of the first century; and (*b*) that the enemies of Christianity tried to refute this Christian tradition by giving a naturalistic interpretation to the facts which it reported.[3]

But the writings of Thallus have disappeared; we know them only in fragments cited by later writers.

[1] The extant fragments of this work are collected in C. Müller's *Fragmenta Historicorum Græcorum* iii, 517 ff., and in F. Jacoby, *Die Fragmente der griechischen Historiker*, II, B (Berlin, 1929), § 256.

[2] In the fourth-century 'Acts of Pilate' (xi. 2) a similar explanation of the darkness is given by the Jews.

[3] *Cf.* M. Goguel, *Life of Jesus*, p. 93.

Apart from him, no certain reference is made to Christianity in any extant non-Christian Gentile writing of the first century. There is, indeed, in the British Museum an interesting manuscript preserving the text of a letter written some time later than AD 73, but how much later we cannot be sure. This letter was sent by a Syrian named Mara Bar-Serapion to his son Serapion. Mara Bar-Serapion was in prison at the time, but he wrote to encourage his son in the pursuit of wisdom, and pointed out that those who persecuted wise men were overtaken by misfortune. He instances the deaths of Socrates, Pythagoras and Christ :

'What advantage did the Athenians gain from putting Socrates to death? Famine and plague came upon them as a judgment for their crime. What advantage did the men of Samos gain from burning Pythagoras? In a moment their land was covered with sand. What advantage did the Jews gain from executing their wise King? It was just after that that their kingdom was abolished. God justly avenged these three wise men: the Athenians died of hunger; the Samians were overwhelmed by the sea; the Jews, ruined and driven from their land, live in complete dispersion. But Socrates did not die for good; he lived on in the teaching of Plato. Pythagoras did not die for good; he lived on in the statue of Hera. Nor did the wise King die for good; He lived on in the teaching which He had given.'

This writer can scarcely have been a Christian, or he would have said that Christ lived on by being raised from the dead. He was more probably a Gentile philosopher, who led the way in what later became a commonplace—the placing of Christ on a comparable footing with the great sages of antiquity.

The reason for the paucity of references to Christianity in first-century classical literature is not far to seek. From the standpoint of imperial Rome, Christianity in the first hundred years of its existence was an obscure, disreputable, vulgar oriental superstition, and if it found its way into official records at all these would most likely be the police records, which (in common with many other first-century documents that we should like to see) have disappeared.[1]

[1] The 'foreign superstition' with which, according to Tacitus

Justin and Tertullian[1] believed that the record of the census of Luke ii. 1, including the registration of Joseph and Mary, would be found in the official archives of the reign of Augustus, and they referred their readers who wished to be reassured of the facts of our Lord's birth to these archives. This need not mean that they themselves had consulted the archives, but simply that they were quite sure that the records were preserved in them.

We should especially like to know if Pilate sent home to Rome any report of the trial and execution of Jesus, and, if so, what it contained. But it is not certain that he must have done so; and if he did, it has disappeared beyond trace.

Certainly some ancient writers believed that Pilate did send in such a report, but there is no evidence that any of them had any real knowledge of it. About AD 150 Justin Martyr, addressing his *Defence of Christianity* to the Emperor Antoninus Pius, referred him to Pilate's report, which Justin supposed must be preserved in the imperial archives. 'But the words, "They pierced my hands and my feet," ' he says, 'are a description of the nails that were fixed in His hands and His feet on the cross; and after He was crucified, those who crucified Him cast lots for His garments, and divided them among themselves; and that these things were so, you may learn from the "Acts" which were recorded under Pontius Pilate.'[2] Later he says : 'That He performed these miracles you may easily be satisfied from the "Acts" of Pontius Pilate.'[3]

Then Tertullian, the great jurist-theologian of

(*Annals* xiii. 32), Pomponia Græcina, the wife of Aulus Plautius, the conqueror of Britain, was charged in AD 57, was probably Christianity. Christianity, too, seems to have been the crime for which the Emperor Domitian had his cousin Flavius Clemens executed and the latter's wife Flavia Domitilla banished, AD 95 (Suetonius, *Life of Domitian* xv. 1; Dio Cassius, *History* lxvii. 14). When the accused were distinguished enough, the police records became part of the stuff of history. The probability that both Pomponia and Flavia Domitilla were Christians is supported by the evidence of early Christian cemeteries in Rome. *Cf.* F. F. Bruce, *The Spreading Flame*, pp. 137 f., 162 ff.

[1] Justin, *Apol.* i. 34; Tert., *adv. Marc.* iv. 7, 19.
[2] *Apol.* i. 35.   [3] *Apol.* i. 48.

Carthage, addressing his *Defence of Christianity* to the Roman authorities in the province of Africa about AD 197, says: 'Tiberius, in whose time the Christian name first made its appearance in the world, laid before the Senate tidings from Syria Palestina which had revealed to him the truth of the divinity there manifested, and supported the motion by his own vote to begin with. The Senate rejected it because it had not itself given its approval. Cæsar held to his own opinion and threatened danger to the accusers of the Christians.'[1]

It would no doubt be pleasant if we could believe this story of Tertullian, which he manifestly believed to be true; but a story so inherently improbable and inconsistent with what we know of Tiberius, related nearly 170 years after the event, does not commend itself to a historian's judgment.

When the influence of Christianity was increasing rapidly in the Empire, one of the last pagan emperors, Maximin II, two years before the Edict of Milan, attempted to bring Christianity into disrepute by publishing what he alleged to be the true 'Acts of Pilate', representing the origins of Christianity in an unsavoury guise. These 'Acts', which were full of outrageous assertions about Jesus, had to be read and memorized by school-children. They were manifestly forged, as Eusebius the historian pointed out at the time;[2] among other things, their dating was quite wrong, as they placed the death of Jesus in the seventh year of Tiberius (AD 20), whereas the testimony of Josephus[3] is plain that Pilate did not become procurator of Judæa till Tiberius' twelfth year (not to mention the evidence of Luke iii. 1, according to which John the Baptist began to preach in the fifteenth year of Tiberius). We do not know in detail what these alleged 'Acts' contained, as they were naturally suppressed on Constantine's accession to power; but we may surmise that they had some affinity with the *Toledoth Yeshu,* an anti-Christian compilation popular in some Jewish circles in mediaeval times.[4]

Later in the fourth century another forged set of

---

[1] *Apol.* v. 2.   [2] Eusebius, *Hist. Eccl.* i. 9.   [3] *Antiquities* xviii. 2. 2.
[4] *Cf.* Klausner, *Jesus of Nazareth,* pp. 47 ff.

'Acts of Pilate' appeared, this time from the Christian side, and as devoid of genuineness as Maximin's, to which they were perhaps intended as a counterblast. They are still extant, and consist of alleged memorials of the trial, passion, and resurrection of Christ, recorded by Nicodemus and deposited with Pilate. (They are also known as the 'Gospel of Nicodemus'.) A translation of them is given in M. R. James' *Apocryphal New Testament,* pp. 94 ff., and they have a literary interest of their own, which does not concern us here.

The greatest Roman historian in the days of the Empire was Cornelius Tacitus, who was born between AD 52 and 54 and wrote the history of Rome under the emperors. About the age of sixty, when writing the history of the reign of Nero (AD 54-68), he described the great fire which ravaged Rome in AD 64 and told how it was widely rumoured that Nero had instigated the fire, in order to gain greater glory for himself by rebuilding the city. He goes on :

'Therefore, to scotch the rumour, Nero substituted as culprits, and punished with the utmost refinements of cruelty, a class of men, loathed for their vices, whom the crowd styled Christians. Christus, from whom they got their name, had been executed by sentence of the procurator Pontius Pilate when Tiberius was emperor; and the pernicious superstition was checked for a short time, only to break out afresh, not only in Judæa, the home of the plague, but in Rome itself, where all the horrible and shameful things in the world collect and find a home.'[1]

This account does not strike one as having been derived from Christian sources nor yet from Jewish informants, for the latter would not have referred to Jesus as Christus. For the pagan Tacitus, Christus was simply a proper name; for the Jews, as for the first Christians, it was not a name but a title, the Greek equivalent of the Semitic *Messiah* ('Anointed'). The Christians called Him Christus, because they believed He was the promised Messiah; the Jews, who did not believe so, would not have given Him that honoured title. Tacitus was in a position to have access to such

[1] *Annals* xv. 44.

official information as was available; he was the son-in-law of Julius Agricola, who was governor of Britain from AD 80 to 84. If Pilate did send a report to Rome, Tacitus was more likely to know of it than most writers; but his language is too summary to make any such inference certain. One point is worth noting, however : apart from Jewish and Christian writers, Tacitus is the one and only ancient author to mention Pilate. It may surely be accounted one of the ironies of history that the only mention Pilate receives from a Roman historian is in connection with the part he played in the execution of Jesus![1]

The Great Fire of Rome is also mentioned by Suetonius, who about AD 120 wrote the lives of the first twelve Cæsars, from Julius Cæsar onwards. In his *Life of Nero* (xvi. 2) he says :

'Punishment was inflicted on the Christians, a class of men addicted to a novel and mischievous superstition.'

Another possible reference to Christianity occurs in his *Life of Claudius* (xxv. 4), of whom he says :

'As the Jews were making constant disturbances at the instigation of Chrestus, he expelled them from Rome.'

It is not certain who this Chrestus was; but it is most likely that the strife among the Roman Jews at that time was due to the recent introduction of Christianity into Jewish circles in Rome, and that Suetonius, finding some record of Jewish quarrelling over one Chrestus (a variant spelling of Christus in Gentile circles), inferred wrongly that this person was actually in Rome in the time of Claudius. However that may be, this statement has another claim on our interest, for we read in Acts xviii. 1 f. that when Paul came to Corinth (probably in AD 50) he found there a man named Aquila, with his wife Priscilla, lately come from Rome, for Claudius had commanded all Jews to depart from Rome. This couple played a distinguished part in early Christian history; they may well have been foundation members of the church in Rome.

[1] There is a reference to Christianity in what may be a fragment of Tacitus's *Histories*, dealing with the burning of the Jerusalem temple in AD 70, preserved by Sulpicius Severus (*Chron.* ii. 30. 6).

A further point of contact between Suetonius' *Life of Claudius* and Acts is the statement in the former (xviii. 2) that Claudius' reign was marked by 'constant unfruitful seasons' (*assiduæ sterilitates*), which reminds us of the prophecy of Agabus in Acts xi. 28, 'that there should be great dearth throughout all the world; which came to pass in the days of Claudius.'

In AD 112, C. Plinius Secundus (Pliny the Younger), governor of Bithynia in Asia Minor, wrote a letter to the Emperor Trajan, asking his advice on how to deal with the troublesome sect of Christians, who were embarrassingly numerous in his province. According to evidence he had secured by examining some of them under torture,

> 'they were in the habit of meeting on a certain fixed day before it was light, when they sang an anthem to Christ as God, and bound themselves by a solemn oath (*sacramentum*) not to commit any wicked deed, but to abstain from all fraud, theft and adultery, never to break their word, or deny a trust when called upon to honour it; after which it was their custom to separate, and then meet again to partake of food, but food of an ordinary and innocent kind.'[1]

Whatever else may be thought of the evidence from early Jewish and Gentile writers, as summarized in this chapter and the preceding one, it does at least establish, for those who refuse the witness of Christian writings, the historical character of Jesus Himself. Some writers may toy with the fancy of a 'Christ-myth', but they do not do so on the ground of historical evidence. The historicity of Christ is as axiomatic for an unbiased historian as the historicity of Julius Cæsar. It is not historians who propagate the 'Christ-myth' theories.[2]

The earliest propagators of Christianity welcomed the fullest examination of the credentials of their message. The events which they proclaimed were, as Paul said to

---

[1] *Epistles* x. 96. The last words of the quotation allude to the charge of ritual murder, which was brought in antiquity against Jews (*cf.* Josephus, *Against Apion* ii. 8) and Christians (*cf.* Tertullian, *Apology*, 7, etc.).

[2] For brief examinations of 'Christ-myth' theories see H. G. Wood, *Did Christ Really Live?* (1938); A. D. Howell Smith, *Jesus not a Myth* (1942).

King Agrippa, not done in a corner, and were well able to bear all the light that could be thrown on them. The spirit of these early Christians ought to animate their modern descendants. For by an acquaintance with the relevant evidence they will not only be able to give to everyone who asks them a reason for the hope that is in them, but they themselves, like Theophilus, will thus know more accurately how secure is the basis of the faith which they have been taught.[1]

[1] *Cf.* F. F. Bruce, *Jesus and Christian Origins Outside the New Testament* (1974), pp. 19–31.

SUGGESTIONS FOR FURTHER READING

CHAPTER 1

Bruce, F. F., *First-Century Faith* (I.V.P., 1977).

Davies, W. D., *Invitation to the New Testament* (Darton, Longman & Todd, 1967).

Guthrie, D., *New Testament Introduction* (Tyndale Press, 1970).

Martin, R. P., *New Testament Foundations*, 2 vols. (Paternoster Press, 1975–1978).

Moule, C. F. D., *The Birth of the New Testament*[3] (A. & C. Black, 1981).

Moule, C. F. D., *The Phenomenon of the New Testament* (S.C.M. Press, 1967).

CHAPTER 2

Bruce, F. F., *The Books and the Parchments*[3] (Pickering & Inglis, 1963).

Kenyon, F. G., *Our Bible and the Ancient Manuscripts*[5] (Eyre & Spottiswoode, 1958).

Metzger, B. M., *The Text of the New Testament*[2] (O.U.P., 1968).

Robinson, J. A. T., *Redating the New Testament* (SCM Press, 1976).

Sherwin-White, A. N., *Roman Society and Roman Law in the New Testament* (O.U.P., 1963).

CHAPTER 3

Cross, F. L., *The Jung Codex* (Mowbray, 1955).

James, M. R. (ed.), *The Apocryphal New Testament* (O.U.P., 1924).

Souter, A., *The Text and Canon of the New Testament*[2] (Duckworth, 1954).

Wilson, McL. (ed.), *New Testament Apocrypha*, 2 vols. (Lutterworth Press, 1963, 1965).

CHAPTER 4

Dodd, C. H., *History and the Gospel* (Nisbet, 1938).

Dodd, C. H., *The Founder of Christianity* (Collins, 1971).

Higgins, A. J. B., *The Reliability of the Gospels* (Independent Press, 1952).

Higgins, A. J. B., *The Historicity of the Fourth Gospel* (Lutterworth Press, 1960).

Hunter, A. M., *The Work and Words of Jesus* (S.C.M. Press, 1950).

Léon-Dufour, X., *The Gospels and the Jesus of History* (Fontana, 1970).

Manson, T. W., *The Beginning of the Gospel* (O.U.P., 1950).

Manson, T. W., *The Servant-Messiah* (C.U.P., 1953).

Martin, R. P., *Mark: Evangelist and Theologian* (Paternoster, 1972).

Smalley, S. S., *John: Evangelist and Interpreter* (Paternoster, 1978).

Taylor, V., *The Life and Ministry of Jesus* (Macmillan, 1954).

CHAPTER 5

Lawton, J. S., *Miracles and Revelation* (Lutterworth Press, 1959).

Lewis, C. S., *Miracles* (Bles, 1947).

Richardson, A., *The Miracle Stories of the Gospels* (S.C.M. Press, 1941).

Wallace, R. S., *The Gospel Miracles* (Oliver & Boyd, 1960).

CHAPTER 6

Bruce, F. F., *The Epistle of Paul to the Romans* (Tyndale Press, 1963).

Bruce, F. F., *Paul: Apostle of the Free Spirit* (Paternoster Press, 1977).

Dibelius, M., *Paul* (Longmans, 1953).

Ellis, E. E., *Paul and his Recent Interpreters* (Eerdmans, 1961).

Hunter, A. M., *Interpreting Paul's Gospel* (S.C.M. Press, 1954).

Hunter, A. M., *Paul and his Predecessors*[2] (S.C.M. Press, 1961).

Kim, S., *The Origin of Paul's Gospel* (Mohr, Tübingen, 1981).

Machen, J. G., *The Origin of Paul's Religion* (Eerdmans, 1947).

Munck, J., *Paul and the Salvation of Mankind* (S.C.M. Press, 1959).

CHAPTER 7

Barrett, C. K., *Luke the Historian in Recent Study* (Epworth Press, 1961).

Cadbury, H. J., *The Book of Acts in History* (A. & C. Black, 1955).

Marshall, I. H., *Luke: Historian and Theologian* (Paternoster Press, 1970).

Marshall, I. H., *The Acts of the Apostles* (IVP, 1980).

Ramsay, W. M., *St. Paul the Traveller and Roman Citizen*[14] (Hodder & Stoughton, 1920).

Ramsay, W. M., *The Bearing of Recent Discovery on the Trustworthiness of the New Testament* (Hodder & Stoughton, 1915).

Smith, J., *The Voyage and Shipwreck of St. Paul*[4] (Longmans, 1880).

CHAPTER 8

Black, M., *The Scrolls and Christian Origins* (Nelson, 1961).

Blaiklock, E. M., *The Century of the New Testament* (I.V.P., 1962).

Bruce, F. F., *New Testament History* (Oliphants, 1970).

Bruce, F. F., *Second Thoughts on the Dead Sea Scrolls*[3] (Paternoster Press, 1966).

Deissmann, G. A., *Light from the Ancient East*[4] (Hodder & Stoughton, 1927).

Mowry, L., *The Dead Sea Scrolls and the Early Church* (University of Chicago Press, 1962).

Rowley, H. H., *The Dead Sea Scrolls and the New Testament* (S.P.C.K., 1957).

Thompson, J. A., *The Bible and Archaeology*[2] (Eerdmans, 1981).

van Unnik, W. C., *Newly Discovered Gnostic Writings* (S.C.M. Press, 1958).

Yamauchi, E. M., *The Archaeology of New Testament Cities in Western Asia Minor* (Pickering and Inglis, 1980).

CHAPTER 9

Grant, F. C., *Ancient Judaism and the New Testament* (Oliver & Boyd, 1960).

Klausner, J., *Jesus of Nazareth* (Allen & Unwin, 1929).

Montefiore, H. W., *Josephus and the New Testament* (Mowbray, 1962).

Vermes, G., *Jesus the Jew* (Collins, 1973).

Williamson, G. A. (trans.), Josephus: *The Jewish War* (Penguin Classics, 1959).

CHAPTER 10

Barrett, C. K., *The New Testament Background* (S.P.C.K., 1957).

Bruce, F. F., *Jesus and Christian Origins Outside the New Testament* (Hodder & Stoughton, 1974).

Grant, F. C., *Roman Hellenism and the New Testament* (Oliver & Boyd, 1962).

Theron, D. J., *Evidence of Tradition* (Bowes & Bowes, 1957).

Most of the subjects touched upon in this little book are dealt with in entries under appropriate headings in *The Illustrated Bible Dictionary* (I.V.P., 1980), and further suggestions for study will be found in the bibliographies appended to these entries.

INDEX OF NAMES AND SUBJECTS

INDEX OF SCRIPTURE REFERENCES